Lighten Up!

*Confronting the darkness
with Christian character*

Leader's Guide
10 Complete Lessons

Jan Johnson

STANDARD
PUBLISHING
Cincinnati. Ohio

D1418323

Edited by Theresa Hayes
Cover design by Brian Fowler

The Standard Publishing Company, Cincinnati, Ohio.
A division of Standex International Corporation.

© 1999 by The Standard Publishing Company.
Printed in the United States of America

ISBN 0-7847-7068-9

Contents

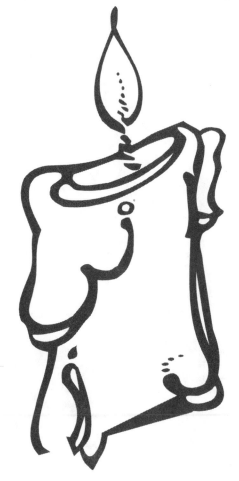

Introduction

Whether your group meets in a classroom at the church building or in the family room of someone's home, this guide will help you get the most out of your Bible study.

You can use this guide with or without *Lighten Up!*, the companion book written by Mike Shannon, but if you do read the book you'll be even more equipped for leading discussion.

Each section of this guide includes two plans—one for classes and one for small groups. This gives you several options:

- Use the plan just as it is written. If you teach an adult Sunday school or an elective class, use Plan One. If you lead a small group, use Plan Two.

- Perhaps you teach a Sunday school class that prefers a small group style of teaching. Use the discussion questions and activities in Plan Two, but don't overlook the great ideas presented in Plan One. Mix and match the two plans to suit your class.

- Use the best of both plans. Perhaps you could start off your class with a discussion activity in Plan Two, and then use the Bible-study section in Plan One. Use the accountability group suggestions, worship ideas, or memory verse options presented in Plan Two in your Sunday school class. Use some of the Sunday school activities and resource sheets presented in Plan One in your small group meeting. Variety is the spice of life!

Resource sheets in each session are available for you to tear out and photocopy for your class or group. Overhead transparency masters are also included for most sessions. Use your own creativity as you decide how to make these resources work for you.

This guide has been developed to help you do several things. First, you'll be able to facilitate active and interactive learning. These methods help students remember and put into practice what they learn. Second, you'll help your class or group apply the lessons to their lives. These sessions will help your group members actually do something with what they're studying. Third, we've given you lots of options. Only you know what will work best in your class or group. Finally, support and encouragement are integrated into each session. Learning and application happen best when participants are helping one another. That may mean allowing yourselves to be accountable to one another if your group has built up the trust and caring that accountability takes, or it may simply mean that people are lovingly encouraging one another to continue growing in knowledge and action.

How to Use This Guide

Each session begins with an excerpt from *Lighten Up!* This excerpt summarizes the session at a glance. Use it in your preparation or read it to your class or group as an introduction to a session. The central theme and lesson aims help you understand the main ideas being presented and what outcomes you are looking for.

Materials you might need on hand to conduct your session are listed on the first page of each of the plans.

In both plans, there are three main parts to each session:

- **Building Community:** a warm-up activity or icebreaker question;
- **Considering Scripture:** Bible-study activities and discussion; and
- **Taking the Next Step:** activities or discussion that will help participants apply what they have learned.

In Plan One for classes, the names of activities are listed in the margins, along with the amount of time to allow for each one. Use these times as a guide to plan your lesson and to stay on track as you teach. In most cases, optional activities are listed. Use these instead of or in addition to other activities as time allows.

A number of options are included in Plan Two for groups. Use the accountability-partner option to help the group support, encourage, and hold one another accountable. This works particularly well in a group in which trust has already been gained between participants. Accountability partners can help one another put what they are learning each week into practice. They can pray with and for each other throughout the week. They can "spur one another on toward love and good deeds" (Hebrews 10:24).

Other options include worship ideas and a memory verse. Use these at your discretion to help your group grow in love, devotion, and praise for God and for hiding His Word in their hearts.

Use this guide to help you prepare, but we suggest that you do not take this book to your class or group meeting and merely read from it. Instead, take notes on a separate sheet of paper and use that as you lead your group.

May God bless the efforts of your ministry!

One
Shine Like Jesus

IN THE TRANSFIGURATION, powerful use is made of light and a cloud. In the Old Testament, the Shekinah glory of God was represented by light and smoke. It's appropriate that Jesus is associated with light because light is a mystery. We can never fully understand it and we can never fully understand the nature of Christ.

Scientists today still discuss the nature of light. Sometimes it behaves as if it's made of particles, other times it behaves as if it's made of waves. We know that light can be so bright that we can see it from stars so far away that their distance can't be calculated. And yet light can also be as gentle as the night light in your house. The truth is that light is unique.

—Mike Shannon, *Lighten Up!*

Central Theme: Focusing on how Jesus showed His splendor and divinity in the transfiguration calls forth reverent obedience. Being awed by the truth about Jesus as Savior gives us the courage to obey and reflect His light.

Lesson Aim: Group members will look at the biblical account of Jesus radiating God's glory and consider how they can reflect the light of Christ in reverent obedience.

Bible Background: Matthew 17:1-9

For Further Study: Read chapter one of *Lighten Up!*

Plan One **Classes**

Building Community

Telling a Whopper, 10-12 minutes

Make paper and pencils available and display Transparency 1A, "Wow Experiences." Give instructions such as, "Pick one of the scenarios on the top that's a wow experience you'd like to have. Then, with a partner or by yourself, quickly make up a story that is so incredible no one will believe it. You (or you and your partner) will be the main character(s) in this story. To help you out, some elements of an unbelievable story are listed on the lower portion of the transparency. Include as many of these elements as you wish. If you need to write your story down, paper is provided."

Circulate among class members, helping any who need a partner to find one. After a few minutes, have one or two volunteers tell their stories and thank them for their participation. Explain that the outline at the bottom of the transparency closely follows the flow of events in today's Scripture account.

OPTION Ranking Experiences, 5-8 minutes

A simpler version of the activity above is to display Transparency 1A and say to class members, "Help me rate these stunning moments from first to last. You may vote for two items that you think are the best wow experiences. The item with the most votes wins." Tally the number of votes at the end of each item to see which one is the favorite.

Materials you'll need
for this session:
Resource Sheets 1A-1B,
Transparency 1A, pens or
pencils, chalk and
chalkboard.

If you wish, refer to the outline at the bottom and say, "If one of these outrageous events actually happened, would anybody believe us? This is, in fact, similar to what happened in today's passage."

OPTION **Light Question, 5-8 minutes**

Ask the class members, "When has a display of light—either natural or human-generated—dazzled you?" After a few have answered, ask, "What was so spectacular about it?" Comment on how light seems to dazzle us in a particular way. You may even want to read the introductory quote from *Lighten Up!* again.

Considering Scripture

Stage Directions, 10-15 minutes

Ask class members to turn to Matthew 17:1-9. Have a volunteer read it aloud. Then give directions such as, "This story has all the makings of a hit movie—especially its God-ordained special effects! So imagine for a moment that you are the director for a movie based on this passage, and you need to make notes on the characters, their lines and movement, and the props needed. Let's fill in this chart together. We're looking for 1) what the characters should say (including Jesus, James, John, Peter, Moses, Elijah, voice of God); 2) how characters should act; and 3) instructions for props and special effects technicians."

Draw four columns on the chalkboard like those below and fill them in a verse at a time. Verse one is done for you. Work together as a class and continue with verses 2-9.

Verse	Characters & Lines	Characters & Actions	Props & Special Effects
v. 1	Jesus: lead 3 disciples	P, J, J: go with Jesus	
v. 2			
v. 3			
v. 4			
v. 5			
v. 6			
v. 7			
v. 8			
v. 9			

OPTION **Dramatizing the Passage, 10-15 minutes**

Ask class members to act out this passage. If you've filled out the chart above this will be easier, but they can act out the passage without having filled out the chart. Ask for volunteers for these parts: Jesus, James, John, Peter, Moses, Elijah, voice of God. Explain, "Since special effects are such a large part of this event, I'll assign them to one person. That person can provide the special effects however they wish (saying in words what the effect is, imitating it, acting it out—hiding behind Jesus and waving arms to the side for dazzling light). It's OK to be silly because it will emphasize just how unusual this experience must have been."

When you are finished dramatizing the passage, ask, "How do you think you would have felt if you had experienced this?"

OPTION **Journaling, 8-10 minutes**

Read Matthew 17:1-9 together. Distribute paper and pencils and say, "Write a day-after-the-event journal entry for Peter and John. Pretend you are one of them and tell a) what happened and b) how you responded."

Have a few volunteers read their journal entries and then ask someone to read John 1:3-9 and 2 Peter 1:16-19. Explain that these passages show exactly how John and Peter reflected on the transfiguration experience. Ask for comparisons to the journals your class members wrote. For example, notice if the journals from class members mentioned these things: light shining in the darkness (John 1:5); statements that they were not making this story up, but were actual eyewitnesses to Christ's majesty (2 Peter 1:16); quoting what God said and describing the voice (2 Peter 1:16-18).

Letters to God, 10-15 minutes

Taking the Next Step

Distribute photocopies of Resource Sheet 1A, "Awed Into Obedience." Read aloud the first question and invite class members to respond. These are thought-provoking questions so allow them a few minutes to think.

(Possible responses: God can transform us even when we feel hopeless. God's power is overwhelming. God's power is great. God has promised us a future with Him and He obviously has access to that realm of divine, miraculous, eternal things.)

Summarize by saying, "Being awed by the truth of who Jesus is and the greatness of His power gives us the courage to obey. In this way, we reflect the light of Jesus who is truly the Savior."

From the resource sheet, read the "situations in which awe of God is important." Ask class members to choose one of the situations. Say, "Put yourself in the place of the person in one of the scenarios. Then write a letter to God that reflects how the truths stated in the questions at the top can be of practical help to you." Give class members time to work and then ask them to read their letters. Summarize: "The miraculous way Jesus changed is encouraging when we feel hopeless. God can change us. God can use us. God can encourage us."

OPTION Small Group Discussion, 10-15 minutes

Distribute photocopies of Resource Sheet 1B, "The Splendor of Jesus Demands Our Obedience" and ask a volunteer to read it. Then ask the two questions at the bottom of the sheet. Regarding question 1, note that just trying harder and harder to obey doesn't work well. What works better is to be impressed with who Christ is and to establish a relationship with Christ. In that way, we allow Christ to change us.

(Possible answers to question 2 include: Through prayer, Bible study, meditation, communicating with other Christians.)

OPTION Take-Home Thought, 2-3 minutes

Suggest these two concrete ideas: Go home and continue to meditate on this dazzling picture of Christ; come back for each of our sessions with a heart ready to hear what God is saying to you at this time.

OPTION: You may wish to use Resource Sheet 1B as an introductory activity to "Letters to God" or as an activity by itself.

Plan Two **Groups**

Building Community

1. Tell about a time when you were awed into obedience. For example, perhaps you had a teacher when you were young whom you adored. Whatever she (or he) said, you did! Or you may have had a kind neighbor or a boss when you were a teen.

Reproducible sheets:
Resource Sheet 1B
(optional)

2. Why is it easier to obey someone we admire or someone we're sure is better than we are in some way?

OPTION: If you have time, use this as well.

3. What story about Jesus most inspires you? What biblical story most puts you in awe of God—that good sort of fear and respect?

Considering Scripture

Read Matthew 17:1-9. If you have time, include the optional questions below. If not, stick with the basic questions.

1. (optional) Why do you think Jesus took only three of the twelve disciples with Him?
2. How did Jesus' physical appearance change?
3. (optional) With what, if anything, could you compare Jesus' brilliant appearance?
4. How did these outward changes make known the inward person of Jesus?
5. Why do you think Peter wanted to build shelters on the mountain top? (Option: Use Resource Sheet 1B, "The Splendor of Jesus Demands Our Obedience.")
6. How did the voice from the cloud confirm the dazzling appearance the disciples had just seen?
7. What did the disciples do when they heard the voice?
8. How did Jesus go about reassuring the disciples in their fear?
9. What had disappeared by the time they looked up?
10. Why do you think Jesus told them not to repeat what they'd seen until the resurrection?
11. (optional) Put yourself in the place of Peter. How did the transfiguration have anything to do with what had happened six days before? *(Look in Matthew 16:21-28. Peter was afraid for Jesus to die, but the transfiguration established Jesus' divinity.)*

Taking the Next Step

1. How do you think this dazzling transfiguration experience with Jesus gave John and Peter the courage to obey later in their lives when:
    a. John lived in exile on the island of Patmos and faithfully wrote Revelation?
    b. Peter stood up in front of a huge crowd at Pentecost and preached although he was not a learned person?
2. In what sorts of situations do people need the courage to obey and reflect Christ in some way?
3. What detail of this passage most impressed you? Picture it again vividly. How can that detail give you courage to obey when you need it?

OPTION **Accountability Partners**

Have partners meet and discuss ways the dazzling presence of God and truth of who He is can help them obey.

OPTION **Worship Ideas**

Read Psalm 43 together as an act of worship.
Song Suggestions:
"Shine, Jesus Shine" by Graham Kendrick
"Righteous One" by Bruce & Teresa Muller copyright 1991, Maranatha Music

OPTION **Memory Verse**

While he was still speaking, a bright cloud enveloped them, and a voice from the clouds said, "This is my Son, whom I love; with him I am well pleased. Listen to him!" (Matthew 17:5).

Awed Into Obedience

What does this vision of a transformed Jesus tell us about ourselves?

... about how God can transform us?

... about God's power?

... about our future with God?

SITUATIONS IN WHICH AWE OF GOD IS IMPORTANT

How do these truths help you when

... you have tried hard to do something right (be nice to a grouchy neighbor, overcome a destructive habit, find a good job) but you keep failing?

... people around you either believe in a different sort of religion or they don't believe in anything at all and they think your faith is obsolete, useless and misguided?

... you have a friend dying of cancer and you desperately want to believe in Heaven, but it's so hard to believe that this flesh and blood friend whose body is diseased will live again—anywhere?

Dear God . . .

The Splendor of Jesus Demands Our Obedience

Peter was so excited about the transfiguration that he said, "If you wish, I will put up three shelters—one for you, one for Moses, and one for Elijah." At that point, a great cloud enveloped them and the voice of God said, "This is my Son, whom I love. . . . Listen to him" (Matthew 17:4, 5). The literal translation is, "Keep on listening to him."

Peter didn't want that moment to end. And if you've ever had a high spiritual moment, you know how he felt. You want to stay in the clouds instead of going down the valley. But in the valley, people are hurting. When Jesus and the three disciples came down from that mount of transfiguration, they found waiting for them a man with a sick son, needing the healing hand of Jesus. Also waiting for them was the cross of Calvary yet to come. But Peter didn't want to go down there. He wanted to stay at that high moment as long as he could. But the truth is that we have those high moments to prepare us to go to the valley and meet the needs of others.

Years ago when I was a college student on a camp team, I served at a camp where vespers services were held high up on the hill in the late afternoon. At this service, people spontaneously testified and so this one hour service might turn into a three hour service. Once, we actually missed our supper because nearly every camper had given some sort of testimony. In the closing prayer circle that night, the leader said, "I think it's time for us to go off this hill back down to the valley. What would have happened to Jesus and Peter, James and John if they had stayed on the mountain?" The camper standing next to me leaned over and said, "They would have starved to death."

There is a time to get off the mountain and to meet the needs of others. We can't lose sight of the hurting people in the world. In our world, there will also be a road that leads to Calvary. In spite of Peter's objection, there will be a cross and death. There will be darkness at mid-day. And there will even be some people who think they have snuffed out that light forever. They couldn't be more wrong. For we know that the light re-emerges stronger than ever. From Calvary the eternal light and life of Christ shines more brightly than ever before.

—Mike Shannon, *Lighten Up!*

How does being on the mountain equip us to meet the needs of others in the valley?

How do we keep on listening to Jesus?

"Wow" Experiences

- Seeing a movie star
- Meeting an achiever in your field
- Meeting a famous musician, artist, or author
- Getting an award from a prestigious organization
- Getting to view a famous comet/ seeing the aurora borealis
- Getting to watch (or participate in!) brain surgery

ELEMENTS TO INCLUDE:

For some reason, you get asked to come along for an event.

Once you get there, it's so much more astounding than you expected. (Include outrageous descriptive details of what happened that astounded you.)

In the midst of it all, you make a suggestion that seems pretty silly, in hindsight.

Just as you're thinking about how you can brag about this, you are told that you can't tell anyone about it. How do you feel?

Two
Follow Like Matthew

MATTHEW'S FIRST ACT as a disciple was to invite his friends over to his house to meet Jesus. Matthew was a tax collector and was therefore considered by most to be a traitor and a thief. Some of the people he invited to dinner were also tax collectors and the rest of the guests were equally considered by the Pharisees to be "sinners." What kind of sinners they were, we have no way of knowing, but the Pharisees were outraged that Jesus would socialize with people of this type.

Some would argue that Christians today need to separate themselves from the world, but if you take that too far, how would any new conversions ever be made? We should separate ourselves from the world in the sense that we don't buy into the world's system, the world's priorities, or the world's values. But even as we deny these worldly things, we must turn around and take the Gospel to people the people of the world.

—Mike Shannon, *Lighten Up!*

Central Theme: Jesus has a caring heart for sinners, even when religious people do not.

Lesson Aim: Group members will look at how Jesus interacted with sinners, explore what it means to view people's hearts as Jesus did, and consider ways to follow Jesus' openhearted model.

Bible Background: Luke 5:27-32; Matthew 9:9-13

For Further Study: Read Chapter 2 of *Lighten Up!*

Plan One # Classes

Building Community

Materials you'll need for this session:
Resource Sheets 2A-2B, Transparency 2, pens or pencils, chalk and chalkboard

Brainstorming, 5-8 minutes

Write at the top of the chalkboard, "Too Tough." Then write the numbers 1-10 vertically down the side of the board. Say to class members, "The world is full of evil people who need the Lord, but whom you and I do *not* wish to talk to. Let's list those really tough cases on the board. Who are the people that you would *least* like to talk to about God? Let's try for ten names. We'll start with . . ." Begin the list with a notorious felon—even a murderer—perhaps in your area. If class members have difficulty coming up with names, suggest world terrorists, foul-mouthed radio personalities, and hardhearted neighbors.

Close by saying, "The only thing more intimidating than talking to the people on this list about God might be talking to them along with ten or fifteen of their friends. Yet that is exactly what we find Jesus doing in today's passage."

Can of Worms Case Study, 5-8 minutes

Explain to class members, "Let's say that someone new began attending our group and after a while, we figured out he was a former Internal Revenue Service agent who had been fired for dishonesty. Let's also say that we decided to collect money for an elderly couple to help them re-roof their home. This former agent has offered to collect the money. What would you say? What would you think?"

After class members have had an opportunity to speak, explain that your goal is not to determine the correct response in this situation. God leads in miraculous ways in these touchy situations anyway. Point out that story helps us think about today's passage and how Jesus treated people we would never trust.

Considering Scripture

Setting the Stage, 10-12 minutes

Display Transparency 2, "Setting the Scene," and explain that Levi and Matthew are two different names for the same person. Continue by saying, "Let's use details from these parallel passages to reconstruct what happened."

Point to Scene 1 and ask class members to tell what happened in this scene. (They should give the details of Matthew 9:9 and Luke 5:27, 28.) Point to Scene 2 and do the same (They should give the details from the rest of the two passages.) Differences in the passages you may want to note are: Luke emphasized that the dinner was a banquet; Luke added that the teachers of the law joined the Pharisees and that they complained. In the last verses, Luke added the word, "repentance," while Matthew continued with the "mercy, not sacrifice" statement (vs. 13).

Read and Respond, 10-12 minutes

Distribute copies of Resource Sheet 2A, "How Jesus Sees Sinners" and ask a volunteer to read it. Before the volunteer begins, explain, "As we read this, consider the heart of Matthew. Jesus was, after all, explaining to the Pharisees what He was doing at Matthew's party. If you were a tax collector who had abused the power of your position (and consequently had sinned against God as well), you would know that you had greed in your heart. How would Jesus' words have affected you?"

Have someone read the introduction and first section of Resource Sheet 2A and then ask, "In what ways would you imagine a man such as Matthew might feel sick in his sin?"

Have someone read the second section and then ask, "In what ways would you imagine a man such as Matthew might feel guilty about his sin?"

Have someone read the third section and then ask, "In what ways would you imagine a man such as Matthew might feel hungry for God?"

OPTION Why Me? Journal, 10-12 minutes

After reading the Scripture, read also the FYI box at the bottom of Transparency 2, "Setting the Scene." Then distribute paper and pencils and suggest, "Let's say it's the night of the dinner party at Matthew's house. As Matthew goes to bed, he writes in his journal:

> Why did Jesus choose me? Why not one of the Pharisees? How could Jesus be so eager to meet my friends? How was Jesus so good at diagnosing what is in our hearts—that we're sick and guilty and hungry?

"Now apply these questions to yourself. Write similar questions pertaining to you. Let God and Scripture speak to you about how to answer them."

Allow class members a few minutes and then ask volunteers to read what they wrote. Each time you hear today's central theme—Jesus has a caring heart for sinners—point it out.

Case Studies, 10-15 minutes

Say to the group, "Scripture says that Jesus can read people's thoughts and hearts (Luke 5:22) and He obviously reads our hearts as sinners. In today's passage, we see what Jesus finds when He reads our hearts. Our problems are that we're sick, we're full of guilt and we're hungry for God."

Distribute copies of Resource Sheet 2B, "Reading the Heart." Break into two groups and have half focus on the "Nasty Sinner," and half focus on the "Nice Sinner," answering the questions for each. If time permits, have the groups report their ideas.

OPTION **Culturalizing the Case Study**

Use the questions on Resource Sheet 2B, "Reading the Heart," except have students substitute a notorious villain (either historical or fiction) for "this person."

OPTION **Personalizing the Case Study**

Use the question on Resource Sheet 2B, "Reading the Heart" but have group members substitute "this person" with someone whom they know personally who *couldn't possibly ever* come to know Christ.

Plan Two # Groups

1. Do you agree or disagree with this statement: "Jesus gravitated toward the outright sinners instead of religious people?" Ask those who agree to raise their hands and then ask those who disagree to raise their hands. Ask each group for their reasons.

Follow up with these questions:

2. Based on the way Jesus ate dinner with tax collectors, who were generally greedy and hated people, what unconventional places might you expect to find Jesus if He visited our planet in the flesh today?

3. What sort of people might Jesus collect as disciples, do you think?

(Be careful not to assume that Jesus was drawn to undesirable people because they were undesirable. Andrew was a disciple of John the Baptist and therefore a religious seeker. Jesus was probably drawn to those with a seeking heart and that was the common denominator among all His disciples. Jesus was skillful at detecting that seeking heart even in undesirable people.)

Read Luke 5:37-42. You may also wish to read the FYI box at the bottom of Transparency 2, "Setting the Scene."

1. How does it strike you that Jesus would go looking for a disciple—one of His team of twelve to affect all of church history—at a tax collector's booth?

2. How do you think it might have struck Matthew himself to be chosen as a disciple? (Explain that Matthew and Levi are the same person.)

3. What does Matthew's abrupt behavior in leaving the booth indicate about what was going on inside him?

4. What does it say about Matthew that he was willing to invite his notorious friends to see Jesus?
5. What does it say about Jesus that Matthew felt able to invite his friends?
6. What does it say about Jesus that He accepted the invitation?
7. In Jesus' answer to the Pharisees' question, how did Jesus demonstrate His ability to look on the hearts of people and see their needs? (If you wish you may distribute copies of Resource Sheet 2A, "How Jesus Sees 'Sinners'" to examine those answers more in depth.) Read Matthew 9:13. Explain that this verse follows the same event in a parallel passage.
8. What did Jesus seem to be telling the Pharisees, who specialized in offerings and burnt sacrifices?

Taking the Next Step

1. Read the three questions below to the group and ask each group member to answer one only. If you have time, have them pick a second question to answer as well.
   a) Put yourself in the place of a Pharisee. Who are the people you feel you are wiser than or better than and have perhaps shunned them from the kingdom?
   b) Put yourself in the place of the other disciples. Who are the people God loves, but you're hesitant to approach on God's behalf?
   c) Put yourself in Matthew's place. How do you feel that God knows all about the layers of your sin and still calls you into His family?

2. Who are the people in your life like Matthew (too sinful, too impossible) that God is asking you to look into their heart?

OPTION **Accountability Partners**

Have accountability groups meet during the week to discuss question 2 (under "Taking the Next Step") more in depth. Remind them of the confidentiality of this accountability partner relationship.

OPTION **Worship Ideas**

Read Isaiah 6:1-8 together as an act of worship.
Song Suggestions:
"Amazing Grace" by John Newton
"He Will Come and Save You" by Bob Fitts

OPTION **Memory Verse**

"I have not come to call the righteous, but sinners to repentance" (Luke 5:32).

How Jesus Sees Sinners

Too often, we view sinners (meaning others who sin as well as the sinner within ourselves) as the enemy instead of victims of the enemy. To help us, Jesus gave us these three pictures of sinners.

SICK PEOPLE WHO NEED A CURE

When Jesus said "It is not the healthy that need a doctor, but the sick," He was offering himself as the great physician to help people with this sickness called sin. Both sickness and sin keep us from being effective. When hampered by sickness, we don't think as we would normally think. Our reactions aren't as fast. We don't drive as well. We don't do our work very well. Likewise, sin keeps us from reaching our ultimate potential. Left unattended, sin can lead us into danger just as untreated sickness can make us seriously ill. Your sickness might be a small thing but if you don't get treatment and find healing, it can lead to death. Even a small cut, if infected and left alone, can lead to death. Sin works the same way. Some sins seem small, but when left unattended, they eventually lead to death.

GUILTY PEOPLE WHO NEED MERCY

Sinners are guilty people who need mercy and pardon. Jesus said, "I desire mercy not sacrifice" (v. 13). Only guilty people need mercy. Since we're all sinners and all guilty, we all need mercy. Some of us pretend that we're not guilty of anything, but we know inside that we are. As guilty people, we're in need of a pardon. Guilty people don't have any real freedom. They're always looking over their shoulder because they're chained to their sins and desires. When you're pardoned, though, it's as if you never committed the wrong. All your rights and privileges are restored. You can know true freedom. In our guilt we don't have any real hope of ever living a life of peace again. But once you're pardoned, you're treated as if you had never sinned. Guilty people never know what it's like to really feel clean. I've counseled with people who have said, "I just feel so dirty." But a pardon wipes that away. You're considered totally clean.

HUNGRY PEOPLE IN NEED OF SUSTENANCE

Many tax collectors and "sinners" came and ate with him and his disciples (Matthew 9:10).

The problem the Pharisees had with Jesus was that He shared a table with tax collectors and other sinners. He was, in fact, showing a kind of affection for them! He had compassion for them. That was Jesus' mission—to seek and to save those who are lost. We are all hungry people in need of sustenance from the Lord. But if hungry people don't come to the table, not only do they not get the food they need but they never know real fellowship either. Today, as in Jesus' day, the sharing of a meal is a symbol of fellowship. Matthew brought his friends to the table with Jesus as part of his discipleship. We need to remember that the lost are not the enemy, but victims of the enemy. We need to invite those in the world to join us at the table. After all, that's how we got into fellowship with Jesus!

—adapted from Mike Shannon, *Lighten Up!*

Setting the Scene

MATTHEW 9:9-13

9 As Jesus went on from there, he saw a man named Matthew sitting at the tax collector's booth. "Follow me," he told him, and Matthew got up and followed him.

10 While Jesus was having dinner at Matthew's house, many tax collectors and "sinners" came and ate with him and his disciples.

11 When the Pharisees saw this, they asked his disciples, "Why does your teacher eat with tax collectors and 'sinners'?"

12 On hearing this, Jesus said, "It is not the healthy who need a doctor, but the sick.

13 But go and learn what this means: 'I desire mercy, not sacrifice.' For I have not come to call the righteous, but sinners."

LUKE 5:27-32

27 After this, Jesus went out and saw a tax collector by the name of Levi sitting at his tax booth. "Follow me," Jesus said to him,

28 and Levi got up, left everything and followed him.

29 Then Levi held a great banquet for Jesus at his house, and a large crowd of tax collectors and others were eating with them.

30 But the Pharisees and the teachers of the law who belonged to their sect complained to his disciples, "Why do you eat and drink with tax collectors and 'sinners'?"

31 Jesus answered them, "It is not the healthy who need a doctor, but the sick.

32 I have not come to call the righteous, but sinners to repentance."

Scene 1: Near the tax booth

Scene 2: Later at Matthew's home

Scene 3: Pharisees talking to Jesus

FYI—In an effort to collect taxes as cheaply as possible, the Roman government auctioned off the right to collect taxes and the winner was responsible for an agreed sum. Anything above that was his. This led to grave abuses. People didn't know how much they were supposed to pay anyway and had no way to appeal. Many tax collectors became wealthy through extortion. These men were universally hated, serving their country's conquerors and becoming rich at the expense of their fellow Jews.[1]

[1]Information gathered from William Barclay, *The Gospel of Matthew* Vol. 1, (Philadelphia, PA: Westminster Press), 1958, p. 336-337.

Reading the Heart

"NASTY SINNERS"

Craig is an impossible neighbor. He lets his lawn grow into long weeds. You can hear him abusing his wife and kids day and night. Although he brags about how he's someday going to inherit millions, he seems very unhappy when he sits on his front porch at night and drinks.

"NICE SINNERS"

Karen is a nice person. She volunteers at the hospital and is willing to help others anytime. But she's not a "churchgoer" (as she calls it) and politely refuses to go when you ask.

Sick People Who Need a Cure

How does this person's fault/lack of knowledge of Christ make them ineffective in their job or family or friendships or health?

What might happen if this person's "sickness" is left untreated?

Guilty People Who Need Mercy

In what ways is this person in need of pardon?

In what ways is this person chained to his or her sins and desires?

Hungry People in Need of Sustenance

In what way does this person need for a Christian to seek out him or her, even show affection for him or her?

In what ways does this person need a Christian to show compassion for him or her?

Three
Lead Like Andrew

IN CIRCLES WHERE church growth is studied, people talk about "the web" or the "network principle." They're referring to the fact that people are usually won by their close friends or family. One church conducted a study, asking people, "How did you get here?" They found that in one five-year period, more than twenty-five people had come to the Lord because of one person.

When I first learned of this principle, I decided to examine it in my own Sunday school class. The class I was teaching at the time had about thirty-five students. I asked them, "How did you get to this church?" They started telling their stories and we found only two couples in that class had not been invited by somebody else—one was my wife and me and we had been hired to come there. Nearly all of them came because close friends or family had invited them.

—Mike Shannon, *Lighten Up!*

Central Theme: Andrew demonstrated specific qualities that can help people tell others about Jesus: being clear about his convictions, unafraid to share the gospel with friends and relatives, unwilling to argue people into the kingdom, and unafraid to take a back seat.

Lesson Aim: Group members will examine Andrew's behavior in telling others about Jesus and explore how they can imitate that in their lives.

Bible Background: John 1:35-42

For Further Study: Read Chapter 3 of *Lighten Up!*

Plan One **Classes**

Top 10 Worst List, 5-7 minutes

Say to group members, "Today's session is about telling others about Christ. Quickly, let's form a top 10 list of the worst things to do when telling others about Christ." Don't bother to write these on the chalkboard. Let class members simply come up with ideas—the more outrageous, the better because this helps us see ourselves better.

If any of their suggestions resemble the mistakes mentioned on Resource Sheet 3B, "What Andrew Did Right," make a mental note of that and refer to it later when the resource sheet is used.

OPTION **Pantomime, 5-7 minutes**

Say to group members, "Today's session is about telling others about Christ. It would be easy to come up with a list of the worst things you could do when telling others about Christ, but I want to challenge you to do this instead. Think of a terrible thing to do when trying to tell someone about Christ and then come up here and act it out without saying a word."

Building Community

Materials you'll need for this session: Resource Sheets 3A-3B, Transparency 3, pens or pencils, chalk and chalkboard.

Thank each one who participates and then ask, "How would you describe what you were acting out?"

Considering Scripture

Graphic Storyboard, 10-15 minutes

Distribute pencils and photocopies of Resource Sheet 3A, "Getting Into the Passage." Have a volunteer read John 1:35-42 (which is on the sheet) and then point out how the first square is filled out. Explain, "JtB" stands for John the Baptist; "A" stands for Andrew; and "X" stands for the other disciple who is not named. The first square illustrates verse 35 in which the two disciples are listening to John the Baptist.

After explaining this say, "Complete the other squares of the storyboard, charting the interaction of the characters as is done in the first square. This helps us plainly see Andrew's role. If you don't wish to use all seven squares, you don't have to."

Allow class members a few minutes. When they're finished, it might look something like this:

v. 35	v. 36	v. 37	v. 38

v. 39	v. 40	v. 41	v. 42

OPTION Interview with Peter, 10-15 minutes

After today's Scripture passage is read, distribute copies of Resource Sheet 3B, "What Andrew Did Right." Ask class members to form pairs, with one taking the role of Peter and the other taking the role of a television interviewer. Explain, "Imagine that Peter is being interviewed on a television show later in life. The interviewer's primary questions are, 'How did your brother bring you to Christ? What did Andrew do right?'" Read Resource Sheet 3B together and rehearse an interview that answers these questions, using material from the sheet.

Allow class members a few minutes. Help anyone having trouble finding a partner do so. Circulate among them, asking those who are catching on to present their interviews to the entire class.

OPTION Paraphrase, 10-12 minutes

Distribute copies of Resource Sheet 3A, "Getting Into the Passage," and ask a volunteer to read today's passage printed at the top. As a class, read together Resource Sheet 3B, "What Andrew Did Right." Ask the class to paraphrase each of today's verses on the bottom of Resource Sheet 3A. Tell them to put it in modern language and update images if they wish (e.g. "Lamb of God"). Tell them to emphasize the tone of the four things that Andrew did right. Allow them to work with a partner if they wish to.

Allow class members a few minutes and then ask a few class members to read their paraphrases.

Open-Ended Stories, 10-15 minutes

Display Transparency 3, "Unfinished Episodes." Read the first unfinished story and ask class members to suggest an appropriate response or action and then an inappropriate one. Don't be satisfied with cut and dried responses. Offer these examples if you wish. "Take Melinda, for example. She may need to take a back seat, but that doesn't mean she isn't powerfully involved in praying for this guest or that she can't be there to listen and reflect back to the guest." If only one answer is given, keep asking, "What else is appropriate/inappropriate?" You may want to say, "Don't limit your responses to concrete actions. What attitudes of the heart are appropriate or inappropriate?"

OPTION Question Box, 5-20 minutes

Before class, put half-sheets of paper on each chair. Explain, "As we talk today, you may start thinking about troublesome situations in your life with people you want to talk to about Christ, but it's not happening. On your sheet of paper, write at least one question to ask about that situation. For example, 'What can I do to avoid getting angry at the person who won't listen to me?' Write your questions on the sheet of paper and fold it. Later, I'll pass a basket and collect them."

Later, pass the basket. Don't ask if anyone has a question because some will be reluctant to speak up. Simply pass the basket and see if questions are submitted. If so, present them to the class and ask for input.

OPTION Self-Evaluation and Prayer, 5-7 minutes

If you haven't already distributed photocopies of Resource Sheet 3B, "What Andrew Did Right," do so now. Say to class members, "Circle the one or two things Andrew did right that you most need to consider. If you wish, turn the sheet over and write a prayer to God about how you think He is leading you in this matter."

Plan Two **Groups**

Building Community

Reproducible sheets:
(optional) Resource Sheet 3B

Take a survey, asking, "Who in your life was most responsible for introducing you to Christ?" Keep a tally:

Those introduced to Christ by relatives _____

By a friend _____

By a stranger _____

Other:

OPTION

Read the paragraph from *Lighten Up!* at the beginning of this study about the network principle and compare your group's statistics to those. Were all of your group members invited by someone else?

OPTION

1. Who in your life has best shown you what life in Christ is like?
2. Who have you known who has been best at introducing people to Christ?

Considering Scripture

Read John 1:35-42.

1. What do we know about these two "disciples"? *(Look for clues in the ministry of John the Baptist. See Matthew 3:1-5.)*

2. What did John the Baptist mean by calling Jesus, "the Lamb of God"? *(See John 1:29, Revelation 7:17.)*

3. What was John's relationship to Jesus? *(See John 1:26, 27, 29-34; Luke 1:36-38.)*

4. How do you explain Jesus' question of the two disciples, "What do you want?" (If you wish, distribute photocopies of Resource Sheet 3B, "What Andrew Did Right," and ask someone to read the section titled, "We Need To Get Clear About Our Own Convictions.")

5. What seemed to be Jesus' method of discipling these two followers of John?

6. What was Andrew's first response to spending time with Jesus?

7. What was the simple message Andrew delivered to Peter about Jesus? (Note the paraphrase on Resource Sheet 3B in the section titled, "We can't argue people into the kingdom": "We found Him. Check it out for yourself.")

8. Jesus exhibited unusual familiarity with Peter by giving him a new name (or nickname), Cephas. How do you explain that quick friendship?

9. From what you know of Scripture and history, which brother went on to take a back seat in terms of attention paid to him?

Taking the Next Step

1. In which of these ways is Andrew an important example for you?
   - Clear about his convictions
   - Unafraid to share the gospel with friends and relatives
   - Unwilling to argue people into the kingdom
   - Unafraid to take a back seat

2. What do you need to think or feel or do or be to have attitudes like Andrew?

3. Who are the people whom you most desire to hear the gospel message in a clear, helpful way?

OPTION **Accountability Partners**

Have accountability groups meet during the week to discuss questions 2 and 3 under "Taking the Next Step" in a more in-depth manner. Encourage them to pray for the persons listed in answer to question 3.

OPTION **Worship Ideas**

Read Romans 10:8-15 together as an act of worship.
Song Suggestions:
"Nothing But the Blood" by Robert Lowry
"Go Forth" by Mark Altrogge

OPTION **Memory Verse**

The first thing Andrew did was to find his brother Simon and tell him, "We have found the Messiah" (that is, the Christ) (John 1:41).

Getting Into the Passage

35 The next day John was there again with two of his disciples.

36 When he saw Jesus passing by, he said, "Look, the Lamb of God!"

37 When the two disciples heard him say this, they followed Jesus.

38 Turning around, Jesus saw them following and asked, "What do you want?" They said, "Rabbi" (which means Teacher), "where are you staying?"

39 "Come," he replied, "and you will see." So they went and saw where he was staying, and spent that day with him. It was about the tenth hour.

40 Andrew, Simon Peter's brother, was one of the two who heard what John had said and who had followed Jesus.

41 The first thing Andrew did was to find his brother Simon and tell him, "We have found the Messiah" (that is, the Christ).

42 And he brought him to Jesus. Jesus looked at him and said, "You are Simon son of John. You will be called Cephas" (which, when translated, is Peter).

John 1:35-42

v. 35	v. 36	v. 37	v. 38
JtB ← A, X			

v. 39	v. 40	v. 41	v. 42

What Andrew Did Right

Today we can learn from Andrew how to be that quiet witness, that gentle persuader, that guiding light. If we're going to be guiding lights, then, like Andrew, we need to observe the following principles.

We need to get clear about our own convictions.

Andrew developed his convictions first from John the Baptist who taught him the need for repentance and baptism. John planted the seeds of discipleship in Andrew's life. But when his teacher said Jesus was the "Lamb of God" (v. 36), Andrew went to investigate for himself. Andrew and another of John's disciples followed Jesus until Jesus turned around, looked at them and said, "What do you want?" Literally, this means, "What do you seek? What are you looking for?"

With this one question, Jesus asked Andrew to search his heart. What was he looking for in a messiah? Was he looking for a political messiah to drive out the Romans? Was he looking for a legalistic messiah who would join forces with the Pharisees? Was he looking for a personal messiah who would simply help him deal with his personal problems? Was he looking for a messiah who would give him a place of honor and power and influence? What sort of messiah are you looking for? That's a question all of us have to answer.

Yet, to be clear about our convictions doesn't mean that we won't ever ask questions or have doubts. It does mean that we will commit ourselves to study, learn, grow, and strengthen our convictions.

We can't be afraid to share the gospel with those close to us.

This principle works. Look at Jesus' twelve disciples. They include at least three brother teams: Peter and Andrew; James and John; Matthew and James the Less. Some believe Philip and Bartholomew were brothers, but we don't know for sure. There may also have been a father and son team. One of the twelve was called, literally "Judas of James" (Luke 6:16 in the New *International Version*). The *King James Version* says, "Judas, brother of James" but the word "brother" is not in the original text. It says simply, "Judas of James." Normally we would take that to mean "son of." So the disciples may have included a father and son team. No doubt, many of them were friends and acquaintances. Peter, Andrew, James, and John worked side-by-side in the same business and over on the shore was Matthew, who sat at the tax collecting booth (Matthew 9:9).

Friends and family have always brought each other into the kingdom—no matter how nervous or uncomfortable they were about it.

We can't argue people into the kingdom.

When Andrew first went to Simon Peter he simply said, "We have found the Messiah." Then he beckoned Peter to come and check it out for himself. He didn't get into a debate over the nature of the messiah. He didn't bring out the messianic texts in the Old Testament. He simply said, "We found him. Check it out for yourself." If that's your approach, not many people will be offended.

We can't be afraid to take a back seat.

In the synoptic Gospels of Matthew, Mark and Luke, the only time Andrew is mentioned is in the list of apostles. Only the Gospel of John tells us anything more about Andrew. Some people believe that the other disciple mentioned in John 1:35-40 was John. That may be, because John was hesitant to mention himself in his Gospel. And if that's the case, it's interesting that John made sure Andrew got some mention when he wrote his Gospel.

—excerpted from Mike Shannon, *Lighten Up!*

Unfinished Episodes

Melinda volunteers at a homeless shelter and has been talking to one of the regular guests about life in Christ. It was exciting, but now another volunteer has started a Bible study and this guest raves about the Bible study.

APPROPRIATE RESPONSE/ACTION	INAPPROPRIATE RESPONSE/ACTION

Dan teaches a Bible class and enjoys talking with class members about who Christ is. But talking to his own brother whom he loves terrifies him. What if his brother rejects him?

APPROPRIATE RESPONSE/ACTION	INAPPROPRIATE RESPONSE/ACTION

Curtis is frustrated because although he has great discussions with his Muslim neighbor, he always thinks of a better thing he could have said two hours later. He asked his wife, "So, should I go back over there and . . . ?"

APPROPRIATE RESPONSE/ACTION	INAPPROPRIATE RESPONSE/ACTION

Julie has been talking to a co-worker about Christ. The latest comment he made was that he couldn't believe that crazy story about a flood. Julie wondered, *Uh . . . maybe you can't. Should I be honest and say I'm not sure I do either? Should I skip it? What should I do?*

APPROPRIATE RESPONSE/ACTION	INAPPROPRIATE RESPONSE/ACTION

Four
Work Your Faith

LET'S LOOK AT a few analogies that show how faith and works are in dynamic tension. Can we separate the brain from the spinal column? Technically, yes, we can. You can dissect a body and separate the parts and say, "This is the brain," and "That is the spinal column." But do we want them separated in the physical life we live? No, we want them to stay connected so we can function. The brain needs to send and receive the messages necessary to operate our body. In practical terms, they cannot be separated and still fulfill their function.

Can we separate the heart from the blood vessels? Sure. There's the heart and there's the blood vessels. But in practical terms we don't want them separated because the blood needs to be pumped from the heart through those vessels to do its work.

—Mike Shannon, *Lighten Up!*

Central Theme: Responding to the light of Jesus means letting the faith that is in your heart show itself in outward deeds.

Lesson Aim: Group members will look at a biblical example of faith (shown in an outward way) and discuss how the faith in our hearts can be expressed outwardly.

Bible Background: Mark 2:1-12

For Further Study: Read Chapter 4 of *Lighten Up!*

Plan One **Classes**

Building Community

Materials you'll need for this session:
Resource Sheets 4A-4B, Transparency 4, markers (for the "Not-So-Newlywed Game"), pens or pencils, chalk and chalkboard.

Word Game, 8-10 minutes

Distribute photocopies of Resource Sheet 4A, "What are the Secret Words?" Read the instructions together and ask class members to begin. If you have adults who don't like word games, encourage them to work in pairs to make it more enjoyable. Remind them not to say the answers out loud but to raise their hands to let you know they've got the answers.

If some class members are struggling, tell them the words begin with "F" and "A." If a few finish quickly, give them the extra assignment of checking their answers. Ask if both of the two words they picked fit into this quotation: (write this on the chalkboard) "_____ is confidence in _____." (Answers: 1, 3, 6 = faith; 2, 4, 5 = action)

OPTION **Not-So-Newlywed Game, 10 minutes**

Choose four pairs from your group. The pairs should be either couples or friends. Designate one person in each pair as the "writer" and the other to be the "speaker." Ask them to sit toward the front and give paper and markers to the writer in each pair. Then say to the class, "We're going to play a game similar to television's Newlywed

Game. I'll ask one question of the 'speaker' in each of these pairs. But before that person can answer, the other partner—the 'writer'—has to write down how they predict the speaker will answer the question."

"Here is the question: Will your partner say that he or she is better at faith, or works?" Have the writer jot down his answer. If you wish, define faith as devotion of the heart and works as outward service.

Then repeat the question and ask the speaker how he or she would answer that question. Listen to the answer and then have the writer partner hold up the predicted answer. Do the same with each pair, clapping for each one.

OPTION Circle Response, 3-5 minutes

Ask class members, "If I were to ask someone close to you, would they say that you are better at faith or action?" Listen for the strengths that people see in themselves or in others. These may be helpful later in guessing words for the acrostics.

Summarize by saying, "Today we'll discover that if you are strong in either faith or works, you're probably not as weak as you might think in the other because they are so closely related."

Marking in the Margin, 10-15 minutes

Considering Scripture

Display Transparency 4, "Taking the Pulse of the Event," and explain, "Sometimes we don't take the time to consider the oddness of biblical events at the moment they occurred. Today's passage is such an event. Look at the code on the page and as I read the passage aloud, mark in the margin the code that indicates the emotion that you believed occurred as that moment in the event happened. Use as many as you like for each verse. Not every verse needs a code."

OPTION Exploratory Questions 5-10 minutes

If you wish, follow up with questions such as the following,

What is your favorite moment in this encounter?

Why did it take great faith for these five men to do this? All along the way, they may have asked questions—the questions any of us ask when we're trying to live out our faith. Is this really worth it? What if we look foolish? What will this cost?

Based on their deeds, what would you guess is going on their hearts? Devotion of the heart is matched with the deeds that follow. They must have felt a lot of compassion for their friend.

Sharing Groups, 10-15 minutes

Taking the Next Step

Ask class members to form groups of three or four. (Let them choose people they know. Don't encourage them to make new friends for this activity.) Distribute Resource Sheet 4B, "Our Deeds Reveal Our Creeds," and say, "Take turns letting each group member read and answer the questions. When it's your turn, answer them all at once, but allow enough time for everyone to have a turn."

OPTION Acrostics, 10-12 minutes

On the chalkboard, write horizontally the word, "faith." Spread out the letters and allow space above and below the letters. Then point to the word and ask, "What are some words that show what faith looks like when it's put in action that we can spell using the letters in the word faith? The words you suggest must have an f, a, i, t or h in them, but don't have to begin with that letter." As an example, write the word "care" using the letter "a." Give them time. If they get stuck, other ideas include: "Help," comFort, servIce, assisT.

After you've done that, write "action" across the chalkboard and say, "Let's make another acrostic using the word "action." This time we'll come up with words that indicate faith or devotion of the heart." Write the word "trust" coming down from the t. Give them time. If they get stuck, other ideas include reliAnce, Confidence, belIef, lOve, hOpe.

Sum up by asking, How is action ineffective without faith? How is faith incomplete with action?

OPTION Doodles/Graphic Design, 5-8 minutes

Distribute copies of Resource Sheet 4B, "Our Deeds Reveal Our Creeds," as well as sheets of paper and pencils. Read the sheet together and then say to class members, "Draw on your sheet something that shows the relationship between faith and deeds. You may want to do a simple doodle or you may want to design more sophisticated graphics using arrows, grids, overlapping circles, or right triangles that mirror each other. Decide this first: Are faith and deeds a matter of cause and effect or do they develop in a parallel way? How do you picture the connection and interaction between these two things? You may want to reread Resource Sheet 4B."

Plan Two Groups

Building Community

What do you think is missing most in among Christians today—inward faith or outward works? Why?

Why is it so difficult to show our faith at times?

When has it been a challenge for you to show your faith?

Considering Scripture

Reproducible sheets:
Resource Sheet 4B

Read Mark 2:1-12

What details are given to us to explain why so many people would gather to hear Jesus? *(Besides His reputation for healing, this was His hometown—probably also the home of Peter.)*

What was Jesus' response to the men tearing apart the roof to get to Him? *(See v. 5.)*

Why do you suppose Jesus said to the man, "Your sins are forgiven" when his need for healing was so obvious? *(Perhaps to engage the Pharisees in discussion that would point to His messiahship or because He saw into the man's heart and knew he needed and wanted forgiveness.)*

How do you respond to Jesus' ability then (and now) to read people's hearts? *(See v. 8.)*

How did Jesus prove who He was through His deeds? *(Jesus proved His messiahship through His healing. He understood it was important for people to see outward deeds to document the inward condition of faith—and deity, in His case. This was Jesus' purpose in healing: "that you may know that the Son of Man has authority on earth to forgive sins" [v. 10].)*

What three physical activities did the man who had been paralyzed a few seconds before do? *(See v. 12.)*

If you wish, distribute copies of Resource Sheet 4B, "Our Deeds Reveal Our Creeds."

How did the five men's faith show through their deeds?

Why did their actions show extreme faith? *(They may have questioned whether they should surmount all the obstacles—the crowd, the roof, whether or not they would win Jesus' attention and favor by interrupting Him.)*

If you're using Resource Sheet 4B, what does that phrase, "Our deeds reveal our creeds" mean? *(That what we truly believe is revealed by how we behave.)*

Taking the Next Step

Is faith really faith without action? (If you wish, refer to the supposed baseball fan on Resource Sheet 4B, "Our Deeds Reveal Our Creeds.")

Why is action without deep faith prone to legalism and hypocrisy?

What are other possible problems with having faith without works or works without faith?

What concrete thing could you do to build the weaker link in your life—faith or works?

OPTION Accountability Partners

Have accountability groups meet and ask them to discuss question 4 under "Taking the Next Step." Remind them that what is said in these meetings is confidential. Such confidentiality allows them to fulfill this Scripture: "Confess your sins to each other and pray for each other so that you may be healed" (James 5:16).

OPTION Worship Ideas

Read Psalm 26 together as an act of worship.

Song Suggestions:

"Trust and Obey" by John H. Sammis & Daniel B. Towner

"The Battle Belongs to the Lord" by Jamie Owens-Collins

OPTION Memory Verse

When Jesus saw their faith, he said to the paralytic, "Son, your sins are forgiven" (Mark 2:5).

Taking the Pulse of the Event

Referring to the four men lowering the paralytic into the house while Jesus was preaching, Pastor Mike Shannon says, "I imagine it was a humorous scene to watch them break through the roof. It's interesting that Jesus was absolutely delighted with this, but then Jesus always rejoiced in seeing great faith."

What do you think? Indicate your thoughts by marking each verse below with the following code:

# anger	? confusion	! delight	✓ determination	~ embarrassment
X frustration	• jealousy	∧ pity	/// resentment	O understanding

Mark 2:1-12

1 A few days later, when Jesus again entered Capernaum, the people heard that he had come home.
2 So many gathered that there was no room left, not even outside the door, and he preached the word to them.
3 Some men came, bringing to him a paralytic, carried by four of them.
4 Since they could not get him to Jesus because of the crowd, they made an opening in the roof above Jesus and, after digging through it, lowered the mat the paralyzed man was lying on.
5 When Jesus saw their faith, he said to the paralytic, "Son, your sins are forgiven."
6 Now some teachers of the law were sitting there, thinking to themselves,
7 "Why does this fellow talk like that? He's blaspheming! Who can forgive sins but God alone?"
8 Immediately Jesus knew in his spirit that this was what they were thinking in their hearts, and he said to them, "Why are you thinking these things?
9 Which is easier: to say to the paralytic, 'Your sins are forgiven,' or to say, 'Get up, take your mat and walk'?
10 But that you may know that the Son of Man has authority on earth to forgive sins . . ." He said to the paralytic,
11 "I tell you, get up, take your mat and go home."
12 He got up, took his mat and walked out in full view of them all. This amazed everyone and they praised God, saying, "We have never seen anything like this!"

What Are the Secret Words?

All the blanks below can be filled in with one of two different words. Read these incomplete sentences and try to guess what those two words are.

Belief is truth held in the mind; _____ is the fire in the heart.[1]

—J. F. Newton

Life is made up of constant calls to _____ , and we seldom have time for more than hastily contrived answers.[2]   —Learned Hand

Now _____ is the substance of things hoped for, the evidence of things not seen.[3]   —Paul

Think like a man of _____ ; act like a man of thought.[4]

—Henri Bergson

In the arena of human life the honours and rewards fall to those who show their good qualities in _____ .[5]   —Aristotle

Understanding is the reward of _____ . Therefore seek not to understand that thou mayest believe, but believe that thou mayest understand.[6]

—Saint Augustine

[1]Alfred A. Montapert, *Distilled Wisdom* (Englewood Cliffs, NJ: Prentice-Hall, Inc. 1964), p. 147.

[2, 5]Rhoda Thomas Tripp, *The International Thesaurus of Quotations* (NY: Thomas Crowell, 1970), pp. 6, 5.

[3]Hebrews 11:1, KJV.

[4, 6]Laurence J. Peter *Peter's Quotations* (NY: Bantam Books, 1980), pp. 8, 181.

Our Deeds Reveal Our Creeds

A strong faith also demands that we take personal responsibility and act. The four men in this Scripture passage had a dynamic faith that was not only accompanied by compassion, but also was expressed by action. These men lived out what James taught: "Faith without works is dead" (James 2:20, KJV). Not, "faith without works feels bad," or, "faith without works is sick," but, "faith without works is dead." These men understood the truth that faith has to have legs on it. Faith is a muscular word. Faith is something that demands action on our part. We have often tried to divorce these two concepts: grace versus works; faith versus deeds. We say we're saved by grace and not by works so we leave works completely out. Or, people talk about our responsibilities and forget grace.

The fact is you can't separate these two things. You may discuss them separately, but in practical terms of how life is lived, faith and deeds must come together. Our deeds reveal our creeds. We don't want to be like the Pharisees, who where concerned with their ritualistic deeds. Notice that Jesus never condemned the Pharisees for their deeds in and of themselves. He condemned them for their wrong priorities and wrong motivations. In fact, Jesus commended the Pharisees for their deeds. We, then, need to have deeds that are consistent with our faith.

Besides, what else is anybody going to see—except our deeds? Someone may claim to have faith, but we can't see his heart. All we can see is how that faith is translated into action. We don't have to become hypocritical like the Pharisees, but *we can match devotion of the heart with the deeds that follow;* the fruit that is born from our faith.

Let's suppose somebody claimed to be the greatest baseball fan of all times. We might ask him, "What makes you the biggest fan ever? Do you know more about the game than anyone else? Have you, for instance, memorized all the stats?"

"Nope, they're not important."

"Do you have a favorite team?" we might ask.

"Yeah."

"Is it in the American or National League?"

"Oh, there are leagues?" asks the supposed greatest baseball fan of all time.

"Yeah, there are leagues," we reply.

The more we discuss it, the more we realize this guy who claims to be the greatest baseball fan of all times doesn't know a thing about baseball. He has done nothing that shows he's a fan. He may indeed be a great baseball fan, but all the evidence is stacked against him.

—excerpted from Mike Shannon, *Lighten Up!*

Look at the italicized phrase above, "we can match devotion of the heart with the deeds that follow."

Describe your "devotion of the heart." It might be your sense of loving God. It might be the people you love. It might be the dedication you have to a cause or a form of service.

How do you express "the devotion of your heart" in everyday deeds?

How do you go out of your way to express "the devotion of your heart?"

Five
Grow in Faith and Worship

WHATEVER CRISIS YOU'RE going through, something will give. Some kind of healing will come. God will work. Not every sick person was healed while Jesus was on earth, but there were moments where Jesus performed these beautiful healings with the power of the Father to show us what He wants to do for us spiritually. And yet we are like the Pharisees saying, "Well, we can already see. We're not blind!" To that Jesus replies, "If that's the way it is, then your guilt remains." If the Pharisees had at least admitted their own blindness, they too could have been healed and been enabled to see.

—Mike Shannon, *Lighten Up!*

Central Theme: As people grow in faith in the Christian life, they can choose either to keep growing and worshiping Jesus or to stagnate in hypocrisy and legalism.

Lesson Aim: Group members will contrast the growing person versus the hypocrite and explore how worshiping Christ helps us to continue to be open to Christ.

Bible Background: John 9:1-41

For Further Study: Read Chapter 5 of *Lighten Up!*

Plan One **Classes**

Building Community

Materials you'll need for this session:
Resource Sheets 5A-5B, Transparency 5, pens or pencils, chalk and chalkboard.

Color Association, 3-5 minutes

Say to class members, "When I say a certain set of words, think of the color that first comes to your mind. Here is the first set: hypocrisy and legalism. What colors did you think of?" After a few colors have been given ask, "Why do you think that color came to mind?"

"Let's try it again with another word: worship. What colors did you think of? Why do you think that color came to mind?

"In today's passage, some people will show hypocrisy and legalism and others will show openheartedness and worship. How do the colors we chose show that these concepts are different?"

OPTION Thought Question, 5-8 minutes

Write this question on the chalkboard, "What is in the heart of the legalist?" Before asking this question of the class, give an example of legalism. Create an example of your own or use this one, "The rule at XYZ church is this: *Camp scholarships are given only to children who have attended our church regularly or whose parents are members.* A young gang kid has been coming to the teen youth group for a month, but hasn't come to church yet. A youth sponsor pleads for him to get a camp scholarship, but the youth committee says no because he doesn't fit in the categories of those who qualify."

Don't focus on how to answer that problem or other problems with legalism, but say, "What causes us to become legalistic? Note that we often start out with good intentions to protect funds or people but eventually we lose compassion and wisdom. We stop interacting with God and think we know what's best."

Considering Scripture

Chart Completion, 10-15 minutes

Display Transparency 5, "Tracks of Growth & Hypocrisy" and designate half of the class as trackers of evidence regarding the man born blind (the left column) and the other half as trackers of evidence on the Pharisees (the right column). Then have someone read John 9:1-41 aloud. Say, "Before we look through each section of Scripture for evidence, let's consider what legalism and hypocrisy are." Distribute photocopies of Resource Sheet 5A, "No Light to See Hypocrisy & Legalism" and ask someone to read it. Then work through the Scripture passage again by sections (1-12, 13-33, 35-41) and ask each half of the room to offer the evidence they find in that section.

(Or you can use Transparency 5 as a master to make photocopies. If you do, have class members form small groups of four or five and assign each group the left or right column. Give the groups about eight minutes to work and then ask a group tracking the blind man for their responses. Ask the other groups tracking the blind man for additions. Do the same with the groups focusing on the Pharisees.)

Here are some responses they might suggest.

THE BLIND MAN
• **What he said about Christ:** He testified continually that Jesus healed him (vv. 11, 15, 17, 25, 30). In so doing, he identified Jesus as a healer, then later as a prophet (v. 17) and a man "from God" (vs. 33). Later, he believed in Jesus as the Messiah and worshiped Him (v. 38).

• **How he interacted with Christ:** He consented to the saliva and mud treatment and obediently washed in the pool of Siloam (v. 6, 7). The man didn't resent Jesus for the fact that the healing resulted in his being thrown out of the synagogue. He attentively engaged in a spiritual conversation with Jesus, and was open to belief in the Son of Man (vv. 35-41). He worshiped Jesus (v. 38).

THE PHARISEES
• **Their criteria for helping people:** (See the three restrictions listed on Resource Sheet 5B). They assumed that Jesus wasn't from God because He didn't behave within these parameters: "This man is not from God, for he does not keep the Sabbath" (v. 16).

• **Their response to the miracle:** They showed no joy over the man's healing, but interrogated him (vv. 15-17). They had already decided Jesus was a sinner (v. 24).

• **Their response to the man and his parents:** They doubted the man was telling the truth about having been born blind (v. 18). The Pharisees operated with a closed mind; "for already the Jews had decided that anyone who acknowledged that Jesus was the Christ would be put out of the synagogue" (v. 22). They intimidated the man and hurled insults at him (vv. 28, 34). Even after they kicked him out of the synagogue, they followed him and overheard his conversation with Jesus (v. 40).

Inductive Study, 10-15 minutes

Introduce this activity by saying, "Both the Pharisees and the man born blind interacted with Jesus, but they responded very differently." Ask these questions (and write them on the chalkboard, preferably). "What was the primary difference between the way the Pharisees treated Jesus and the way the man born blind treated Him? What was the primary difference in their attitudes?" Have four volunteers each read about ten verses of John 9:1-41 and then ask the questions again. Give class members some quiet moments to think about this without interrupting them with clues and prodding. You may wish to draw a vertical line on the chalkboard and write "Man Born Blind" on the left and "Pharisees" on the right. When they are finished, use the earlier material about open-mindedness and closed-mindedness and material from the completed chart, "Tracks of Growth & Hypocrisy" to supply thoughts they may not have suggested.

Finish the Story, 10-15 minutes

Form groups of 8-10. Distribute photocopies of Resource Sheet 5B, "A Tale of Two People," and assign each group one of the two columns. Read the setting at the top and then say, "Read the description of your person. Then describe the way this person behaves and how he talks to others. Then describe how he talks to the people in his church with whom he does not agree." Be sure to allow enough time for each group to report. (Caution: Try to stay away from the familiar criticism of pigeonholing any-one who says, "We've never done it this way before," as a legalist. The core issue is being open to seek God, and God may or may not lead us into something new.)

"Notice that in the end the man born blind worshiped Christ. How can continually worshiping Christ keep us from legalism and hypocrisy?" *(We don't assume so quickly that we know the answers because we have spent significant time acknowledging God's greatness.)*

Taking the Next Step

OPTION **Act out the Story, 10-15 minutes**

Have the class form groups of four and distribute photocopies of Resource Sheet 5B, "A Tale of Two People" to each class member. Say, "Act out this story within your group, including a conversation between characters A and B. Each person in your group should take one of these roles: Person A, sidekick or coach to Person A, Person B, sidekick or coach to Person B.

OPTIONAL CONCLUSION **Prescription Writing, 3-5 minutes**

If you've already used Resource Sheet 5B, "A Tale of Two People," then ask class members, "Review the bulleted characteristics again and then turn the sheet over. What steps is God asking you to take to avoid being a person bent on legalism and hypocrisy and instead be a person who grows in Christ and worships Christ?"

Plan Two **Groups**

Building Community

"When have you been appalled by the legalism in a group, a person or a situation?" (Encourage group members to disguise the situation by changing details when describing it, if it is familiar to others.)

When is it easy to become legalistic? *(Anytime we want our way.)*

OPTION

In what areas are we most prone to want our own way?
Why was Jesus so different from legalistic people?

Reproducible sheets (optional): Resource Sheet 5A, "No Light to See Hypocrisy & Legalism"

Considering Scripture

Read John 9:1-12.

Compare what the disciples thought was the source of the man's blindness versus Christ's understanding of it.

What was it Jesus urged the disciples that "we must do" (v. 4)?

Describe Jesus' interesting curative method.

Read John 9:13-33.

What was the primary concern of the Pharisees regarding the man's healing?

Why did the Pharisees assume Jesus could not be from God? (If you wish, distribute photocopies of Resource Sheet 5A, "No Light to See Hypocrisy & Legalism," and have volunteers read aloud the three reasons why the Pharisees were sure Jesus had broken the Sabbath law. Or, if you wish, read them to the class.)

Why did the Pharisees want to speak to the man's parents?

When the Pharisees summoned the man born blind a second time (v. 24) and said, "Give glory to God. We know this man is a sinner," what were they asking the man to do?

Give your impression of the man's short speech in vv. 30-33.

Read John 9:34-41.

Being thrown out of the synagogue was a crisis for a Jewish man such as the man born blind. How do you explain his positive response to Jesus?

How does the man's opinion of Jesus grow? (See verses 17, 25, 33, 38.)

Taking the Next Step

The man born blind was willing to grow. In what ways can we imitate his attitude? *(He didn't allow himself to be intimidated by anyone. He kept restating the facts and examining the facts to look for the truth.)*

In what ways do we too often imitate the hypocrisy and legalism of the Pharisees? (If you wish, use the rest of Resource Sheet 5A, "No Light to See Hypocrisy & Legalism.")

What is needed to be a person who is open to interaction with God instead of someone who assumes he or she already knows all the answers? *(We must get rid of any hidden agenda—the Pharisees had an agenda of holding onto power and keeping control over religion and politics as much as possible. We must be constant listeners to the heart of God.)*

OPTION **Accountability Partners**

Have accountability groups meet and urge them to reveal to one another one area in which they find it easy to be legalistic. Have them pray for one another about this and explore what they can do to be openhearted worshipers of Christ.

OPTION **Worship Ideas**

Read Psalm 86 together as an act of worship.

Song Suggestions:

"More Love, More Power" by Jude Del Hierro

"Majesty" by Jack Hayford

OPTION **Memory Verse**

Then the man said, "Lord, I believe," and he worshiped him.

Jesus said, "For judgment I have come into this world, so that the blind will see and those who see will become blind" (John 9:38, 39).

Tracks of Growth & Hypocrisy

TRACKING GROWTH in the FORMERLY BLIND MAN

What evidence of growth do you find in the man born blind based on:

What he said about Christ

How he interacted with Christ

TRACKING HYPOCRISY in the PHARISEES

What evidence of hypocrisy do you find in the Pharisees based on:

Their criteria for helping people (See Resource Sheet 5B)

Their response to the miracle

Their response to the man and his parents

No Light to See
Hypocrisy & Legalism

The healing of the man born blind helps to shed some light on sin and sickness, but it also helps us see the light about hypocrisy and legalism. When this man was healed you would have thought everybody would have been happy about it. Not the Pharisees. Unfortunately their hypocrisy and legalism gave them very little joy in life.

Why were the Pharisees upset? They were upset because they believed Jesus had broken the law. The law said, "Remember the Sabbath day by keeping it holy" (Exodus 20:8). One of the ways the Jews obeyed this law was by not working. However, the Pharisees and the scribes were the ones who decided what was work and what wasn't. In this particular case, they saw three ways, in their minds, that Jesus had broken the Sabbath law.

First, he used saliva to make mud. That was work by the Pharisees definition. The Pharisees had decided that if you had to spit on the Sabbath, you had to spit on a rock because if you spit on a rock you wouldn't make mud. But if you spit on the ground you would make mud and that was work. So anybody who needed to spit on the Sabbath had to do it on a rock. Jesus didn't do that. He spit in the dirt and made this mud to put on the man's eyes.

The act of using the saliva itself was also work. This seems very unsanitary to us, but even today there are some who think saliva has medicinal qualities. Even more so in Jesus' day, the saliva of a holy man was seen to have medicinal qualities To the Pharisees, saliva was a medicine and they didn't believe you should be medicating on the Sabbath. You could keep people from dying on the Sabbath, but you couldn't try to make them well. So when Jesus applied saliva, that too, was considered a violation of the law.

The biggest problem was that the man got well. That too was a violation of the law because, to the legalists, it was work. Healing someone was definitely work!

They indicted Jesus with three violations of the law as they read it. There was very little joy in these people and very little opportunity to rejoice. The grand jury called the man in and tried to make him answer for the healing. What did he do? Nothing. This shows that hypocrites have little compassion. In this case, the Pharisees indicted the healed man with crimes just because they were angry with Jesus, and threw him out of the temple.

When Scripture says they threw the man out, that means they put him out of the synagogue. He was no longer able to come to the temple or the synagogue to worship. But what had this man done wrong? Nothing.

Because of their anger at Jesus, the Pharisees put this man out. Hypocrisy and legalism not only involves little joy or compassion, but also little objectivity. A healthy skepticism is good, but that is different from bull-headedness. Alger Fitch summarized these events in this manner:

Jesus saw the blind man and said, "I see a need and I will meet it."

The disciples said, "I see a problem and I'll raise it."

The blind man said, "I see an opportunity and I'll accept it."

The Pharisees said, "I see a sign and I'll reject it."

—excerpted from Mike Shannon, *Lighten Up!*

A Tale of Two People

A merger has been proposed between two small churches. Each church is working through the decision-making process. Create a scenario with these two sorts of people.

A PERSON WHO GROWS IN CHRIST AND WORSHIPS CHRIST

- Responds to what he believes is the leading of Christ
- Acknowledges continually that Jesus is a healer, Jesus is Lord, and humbly worships God
- Attentively engages in conversation with God throughout the situation

A PERSON BENT ON LEGALISM AND HYPOCRISY

- Has a limited criteria for helping people
- Experiences little joy over good things that happen
- Is unable to see God at work
- Operates with a closed mind—makes up mind quickly, doesn't examine evidence of situation
- Intimidates and hurls insults at people with whom he disagrees
- Excludes people with whom he disagrees

Six

Praise Like the Healed Leper

IN ABRAHAM LINCOLN'S DAY it was customary for the President to see ordinary citizens who dropped by the White House to plead their causes and tell their concerns. One day, during the worst part of the Civil War, when a woman came to see him, President Lincoln asked, "'How can I be of service to you, Madam?"

The woman answered, "Mr. President, I know you are a very busy man. I've not come to ask you for anything. I simply came to bring you this box of cookies."

There was a long silence and tears overflowed the President's eyes. He said to her, "Madam, I am greatly moved by what you have done. Since I have become President, people have come into this office one after another asking for favors and demanding things from me. You are the first person who's ever entered these premises asking no favor, but bringing a gift. I thank you from the bottom of my heart."

—Mike Shannon, *Lighten Up!*

Central Theme: God calls us to be thankful, but it's so easy to forget or put off giving thanks that Christians need a strong determination to be thankful—just do it!

Lesson Aim: Group members will contrast the normality of nine men not thanking Christ with the one unusual man who did, and explore what it takes to be a deliberately thankful person.

Bible Background: Luke 17:11-19

For Further Study: Read Chapter 6 of *Lighten Up!*

Plan One **Classes**

Building Community

Materials you'll need for this session:
Resource Sheets 2A-2B, Transparency 2, pens or pencils, chalk and chalkboard

Paper Tear, 5-10 minutes

Distribute pieces of paper to each class member. (An 8 1/2" x 11" sheet of paper torn in fourths is the right size.) Write these words on the chalkboard: "thankfulness, the inability to express one's self, procrastination, insensitivity, forgetfulness." Then say to group members, "Take this piece of paper and tear it into a shape that somehow expresses one of the words on the chalkboard. Don't worry about doing this 'right.' You may come up with an unusual idea that will hit the spot exactly for someone else—anything goes!"

Give them a few minutes and expect some bewildered looks. Encourage them not to try too hard, but just do it.

OPTION **Walking a Continuum 5-8 minutes**

"Imagine that in the front of this room is a line spanning from one corner to the other, representing varying degrees of thankfulness." Point to a corner. "In this corner on one end of the continuum would be people who consistently feel thankful to others and to God and consciously try to express that thanks." Point to the other corner. "In this other corner is the other end of the continuum—people who aren't thankful at all—completely oblivious to all that has been given to them and done for them. Perhaps in the middle are those who feel gratitude but don't know how to express it, or perhaps forget to express it. Come and stand on the place that represents where you are in this continuum of gratefulness."

Allow class members a few minutes to get in place. Thank them for being cooperative and getting out of their seats after they were settled in.

Panel, 10-15 minutes

Considering Scripture

Ask for ten volunteers to play the parts of the ten lepers who were healed. Designate one to be the Samaritan. Give them Resource Sheet 6A, "Fact Sheet About Leprosy." Tell them that you are going to interview them regarding their healing experience with Jesus and that their answers should include the details from Scripture. Let them turn to Luke 17 and keep it open. Have someone else in the group read Luke 17:11-19. Display Transparency 6, "Leader's Cue Sheet" so that the entire class knows what's going on.

If your actors have trouble coming up with answers, you might slip them these prompts:

To question 2: As they were going to see the priests.

To question 3: The lepers were evidently familiar with Jesus because they called Him by name and knew He could help them: "Jesus, Master, have pity on us!"

To question 4: All ten were extraordinarily obedient for reasons we can only guess. Perhaps they'd heard about the healing reputation of Jesus and trusted Him. They didn't even say, "Yes, but we can't go near the priests." They just went.

To question 5: You're just not the expressive type. You wanted to put the past behind you. You're a procrastinator so you waited too long and then felt foolish trying to find Jesus. You're insensitive or perhaps even arrogant. In the joy of the moment, you forgot.

To question 7: It could have just been in his personality or perhaps he was shocked that a Jewish teacher would care about him.

OPTION **TV Talk Show Skit, 10-15 minutes**

Have a volunteer read Luke 17:11-19 and then ask for up to nine volunteers to act as healed lepers turned TV talk show guests. You may wish to be the interviewer or choose a class member who likes to be up front.

Use Transparency 6, "Leader's Cue Sheet" as a master to make photocopies and distribute these only to the "host" and "guests" on the show. Instruct the "host" to ask questions from "Leader's Cue Sheet."

You can be more creative with the talk show format than the panel. For example, encourage at least one of the "guests" to answer question five by sounding insensitive since at least one of the ten may have been arrogant—based on human nature.

Also consider these ideas: 1) Have the Samaritan leper waiting backstage and surprise the others by having him come out at question six and describe what he did. 2) Have Jesus waiting backstage. Bring Jesus out and let the others thank Him. If you do either of these ideas, don't alert the other actors involved. Either ask for these volunteers before class, or as the talk show draws to a close. Call on a class member who is a good sport and ask that person on the spot to play the role of Samaritan or Savior.

OPTION Brainstorming, 5-8 minutes

Read the passage together and then say to class members, "Help me come up with at least eight probable reasons why the other nine lepers did not return—based on human nature. Try not to be too hard on these men—they obeyed well. They immediately left to show themselves to the priests with no evidence of healing yet in place."

Taking the Next Step

A Moment of Silence, 5-8 minutes

Distribute photocopies of Resource Sheet 6B, "Thankfulness Requires a Determined Spirit." Ask a few volunteers to read the handout, one paragraph each. If possible, tell a personal story about someone you have neglected to thank. Then say, "It takes resolve and determination to be thankful because it doesn't come naturally to us. Let's pray silently and ask God to bring to your minds the names and faces of a few people we need to thank. Please don't try too hard to think of someone. Just sit quietly and let God bring these people to mind."

After a few minutes of prayer, do one of the following optional activities.

OPTION Thank You Notes, 8-15 minutes

Distribute paper (colored or textured paper would work, or you can purchase thank-you notes) and pens. Ask group members to write a note of thanks to someone to whom they owe thanks.

Give them a few minutes to work. Point out that if the recipient of a note is here today, the note can be hand delivered.

OPTION Hymn Singing, 5-8 minutes

Choose a song or hymn of thanks—perhaps the one on Resource Sheet 6B, "Now Thank We All Our God." Arrange to have accompaniment of some sort—a tape or instrumentalist. Introduce this time of singing by rereading paragraphs 4 and 5 (beginning with, "In a sermon preached at . . .") from Resource Sheet 6B and saying, "Consider your life in a realistic way. Perhaps few things are going well or perhaps many positive things are happening. Either way, let's offer thanks to God for the unchanging way He reaches out to us and gives us benefits we often forget. You may even want to give thanks with great determination in the midst of a trial." Sing the song.

Plan Two Groups

Building Community

Materials needed:
Wall board or writing chart; Resource Sheet 6A, "Fact Sheet About Leprosy;" index cards for each group member

Before class list the following on the board or chart:

  I usually thank people.

  I get sidetracked.

  Thanking people doesn't occur to me.

Begin the session by saying, "Tell us about a time when someone has thanked you and it was especially meaningful." (If you wish, get the group talking by reading the story about President Lincoln in the introduction to this lesson.)

Refer to the list on the board and ask, "How would you describe your skill at showing thanks?"

What are some situations that make it difficult for you to be thankful? *(Someone demands it of you, when others are unappreciative of you, you have experienced a series of troublesome events, or, life is going so well that you forget to be thankful.)*

Read Luke 17:11-19.

Considering Scripture

Before going through the questions below, have a volunteer to read Resource Sheet 6A, "Fact Sheet about Leprosy." Note that the last point about Jewish law has special bearing on this passage.

1. Where did this event occur?
2. Why did the lepers stand at a distance?
3. What indicates that the lepers already knew something about Jesus?
4. Why did Jesus' command, "Go, show yourselves to the priests," not make sense?
5. The fact that they obeyed Jesus' instructions anyway tells us what about the lepers?
6. Describe the behavior of the healed leper who came back to find Jesus.
7. What seems to have been Jesus' response to the other nine not returning?
8. How did Jesus compliment the faith of this "foreigner"?
9. In what ways were the lepers' lives changed by Jesus healing them?

OPTION

In what other circumstances was Jesus unusually accepting of lepers? Look up the passages on Resource Sheet 6A. *(Jesus visited with and ate with Simon the Leper, Matthew 26:6; Jesus touched a leper when He healed him, Matthew 8:2.)*

OPTION

In what other circumstances was Jesus unusually accepting of "foreigners"? (Matthew 8:5-13; 15:22-28; Luke 7:3-9; John 4:1-42, especially v. 40)

Taking the Next Step

1. What has helped you become more thankful over the years?
2. What inner character qualities are needed to be a thankful person?

OPTION

Distribute an index card to each student. Tell them, "Make a list of at least two people whom you would like to thank. After each name write the specific thing they did for which you are grateful, and what you are most thankful for about them."

OPTION **Accountability Partners**

Have accountability groups meet during the week to discuss how they can thank the people they listed on their index cards. Encourage the partners to also thank each other and tell how the others have been helpful to him or her.

OPTION **Worship Ideas**

Read Psalm 107 together as an act of worship.
Song Suggestions:
"Thank You, Lord" by Dan Burgess
"Give Thanks with a Grateful Heart" by Henry Smith

OPTION **Memory Verse**

"He threw himself at Jesus' feet and thanked him—and he was a Samaritan" (Luke 17:16).

Interviewing the Men Who Were Healed

Luke 17:11-19

Have panelists/today's guests introduce themselves as the ten lepers healed on the Judean-Samarian border road.

1. Tell us what happened. (Be sure to use facts from Scripture in your answer.)

2. At what point exactly were you healed?

3. Who was this healer, Jesus? (See v. 13.)

4. Didn't you think this was unusual for you to be commanded to go near a priest? Lepers weren't allowed to go near priests. True, priests could declare you cleansed, but you weren't cleansed yet. Why did you dare to go to the priest?

5. Why didn't you come back to thank Jesus?

6. One of the ten of you did come back—a Samaritan. In fact, he came back, praising God in a loud voice and threw himself at Jesus' feet and thanked him. Does it surprise you that Jesus, a Jewish teacher, would heal the Samaritan too?

7. Why do you think the Samaritan was the one to return?

Fact Sheet About Leprosy

What was it like to be a leper?

Lepers were shunned by polite society. They had to announce their arrival in any town, and their presence to anyone who approached by shouting, "Unclean! Unclean!" People thought leprosy was much more contagious than it really is, which made them afraid to be around those who were stricken. That's why leper colonies were formed. This ailment, which was common yet frightening in Bible times, was a virtual death sentence, but you were dying a little bit at a time. Day by day, the person with leprosy lost feeling in his or her extremities and little by little, became disfigured. People with leprosy often could not bear to look at their own images. They were separated from family and friends. Their only sense of community was with the other lepers.

What is leprosy?

What the Bible describes as leprosy is not just Hansen's disease, which is what we call leprosy today. It also included a whole range of skin illnesses that affected people in the Middle East. Because lepers were isolated from others, it caused people to be afraid. In a sense, it was like the AIDS of its day in that people were greatly afraid of it. No one ever dared touch a leper.

How common was leprosy?

Many in the Bible suffered from this kind of skin ailment—some permanently, some temporarily. Among those who suffered from leprosy were Moses, Miriam, Naaman, Uzziah, and the four lepers of Samaria. In the New Testament, there was a man known as Simon the Leper, at whose home Jesus visited and even ate (Matthew 26:6, Mark 14:3). Of course, we know that Jesus healed lepers on more than one occasion. Jesus even dared to touch them (Matthew 8:3; Mark 1:41; Luke 5:12, 13). On the occasion in our study, he healed ten. Ten men living the horrible nightmare of leprosy were each given a new dawn of hope by Jesus—a new morning, a new life.

How did Jewish law deal with leprosy?

According to the Old Testament law, only a priest could declare a leper to be cleansed because leprosy was a spiritual problem as well as a medical problem. Because leprosy made its victims unclean in the eyes of the law, lepers were unable to come into the temple or synagogue to worship. So, although only a priest could declare you free from leprosy, the priest rarely saw a leper or saw leprosy cleansed.

—adapted from Mike Shannon, *Lighten Up!*

Thankfulness Requires a Determined Spirit

Every day we see signs of ingratitude. Thankfulness just doesn't come easily to us for a variety of reasons:

- We are not expressive
- We procrastinate too long
- We forget in the joy of the moment
- We put the past behind us
- We are insensitive
- We are arrogant

A man who worked in a post office handling letters to Santa Claus noticed one year that after Christmas was over and the new year had begun another letter came for Santa Claus. He thought maybe the child had gotten confused or something, so he opened it and found a thank you note to Santa Claus for all he'd brought. The postal worker said that in all those years thousands of letters had come asking for things but only once did he see a letter of thanks to Santa Claus.

In the same way, there are times that we don't thank God. Maybe we don't because we are going through tough times and thankfulness doesn't seem appropriate. I can't answer why the righteous suffer or why people have to face problems. But if we are going to blame God for every single bad thing that happens, it's only fair that we thank Him for every single good thing that happens too. If you do that, you'll find you have a lot more to be thankful for than you might otherwise have thought.

In a sermon preached at Emmanuel Presbyterian Church in Los Angeles, Gary Wilburn told this story:

> In 1636 amid the darkness of the Thirty Years War, a German pastor, Martin Rinkard, is said to have buried five thousand of his parishioners in one year. He held an average of fifteen funerals a day. His parish was ravaged by war, death and economic disaster. In the heart of that darkness, with the cries of fear outside his window, he sat down and wrote a table grace for his children. It has been translated into English and has become a part of many hymn books. This is what Rinkard wrote:
>
> > Now thank we all our God with heart and hands and voices,
> > Who wondrous things hath done in whom his world rejoices;
> > Who, from our mother's arms, hath blessed us on our way,
> > With countless gifts of love, and still is ours today.

Can you muster that same determination to find something good even in the worst of circumstances?

I read an old story many years ago about Matthew Henry. The Bible commentator was once robbed by highwaymen. He decided to go back to his room and find something he could be grateful for. He started a list with, "I thank You that though I was robbed I was not killed." He continued, "And I thank You that while I was injured, I was not injured greatly. I thank You that while I was robbed of everything I had, I didn't have much on me." Finally, at the bottom, he said, "I thank You that I was the one robbed, not the one doing the robbing."

—excerpted from Mike Shannon, *Lighten Up!*

Seven

Be as Generous as the Widow

NOT TOO LONG AGO, Ted Turner made the cover of *Newsweek* for a gift of over one billion dollars to United Nations charities. I don't want to take anything away from his gift, because that was a generous thing for Ted Turner to do. He could have kept his money. He could have spent it on himself. He could have wasted it.

That same week the news wires also carried a story about a Mississippi woman who gave $150,000 for scholarship money for poor students. She had saved this money throughout years of washing other people's clothes. I believe that woman deserved to be on the cover of *Newsweek* just as much as Ted Turner. The poor widow we read about in Luke 21 also deserved to be on the cover of *Newsweek*.

—Mike Shannon, *Lighten Up!*

Central Theme: What God values most in a gift is the pure attitude of the heart and desire with which you give it, often evidenced by the sacrifice involved.
Lesson Aim: Group members will examine attitudes of generosity and explore what is needed to have those attitudes.
Bible Background: Luke 21:1-4
For Further Study: Read Chapter 7 of *Lighten Up!*

Plan One **Classes**

Building Community

Materials you'll need for this session: Resource Sheets 7A-7B, Transparency 7, pens or pencils, chalk and chalkboard.

Finishing a Funny Story, 8-10 minutes

Display Transparency 7, "What Would You Say Next?" Read each anecdote and ask the questions after each one. After a few minutes of fun, say, "Each of these kids quoted their parents' real feelings. In the second story, it is evident that the woman's giving actions weren't always matched with a truly giving heart. Isn't this a problem we all have from time to time—we give, but our heart isn't in it?"

OPTION Limerick Writing, 5-8 minutes

Write the following on the chalkboard:

There once was a man from _____ (a)
Who had no heart to give _____ (a)
He _____ (b)
_____ (b)
_____ (a)

Then say something like this, "Let's compose a limerick by finishing these lines. All the lines ending in "a" need to rhyme and all the lines ending in "b" need to rhyme.

Considering Scripture

Alter-ego Statements, 15-18 minutes

Have class members form small groups of four or five and distribute photocopies of Resource Sheet 7A, "Fleeting Thoughts." Read the instructions together and say, "There were at least three situations in which the poor widow must have evaluated her decision to give away her last mites. Work together to come up with ideas for what she might have thought in each of this situations. List also the thoughts she must have had in order to choose to give the money."

Give groups a few minutes to work. If time is short, assign only one of the three situations to each group. Here are some examples of comments the groups might offer.

1a. I have so little. How can I give away this money?

1b. I know that if I give this money to God, God won't let me starve.

2a. I should go help my widow friend who just got swindled by the teachers of the law.

2b. I can help her—true—but I'll give my money with a prayer to God that He will use it and not let it be used shamefully.

3a. How can I throw in my two small copper coins, filing right behind these rich people with all that jingling? It's ringing in my ears! I could slip away and no one would realize I didn't give.

3b. God works miracles (e.g. giving manna from Heaven and parting the Red Sea) and God can multiply my small amount of money to do good.

OPTION Expanded Story, 8-10 minutes

Distribute photocopies of Resource Sheet 7A, "Fleeting Thoughts," and blank paper and pencils. Read the sheet together. Then say to group members, "Use the ideas from this sheet to write an expanded version of this story, incorporating the possible thoughts and doubts the widow might have had. You can have the struggle take place entirely in her mind, or you might want to write it as a script between the widow and a friend or her daughter-in-law."

OPTION Thought Question, 3-5 minutes

Say to class members, "Jesus often made statements that startled His disciples. His observation that the woman put in 'more than all the others' must have amazed the disciples as they watched the rich people throw in so much money. What do you think He meant by that? In what ways was that true? Draw from what you know about Jesus and how He interacted with people."

Give class members a few moments to think. If you wish, prod them with these comments:

Jesus was good at seeing into people's hearts (Mark 2:8). What attitudes of the heart did He see inside this woman? *(He probably saw a heart of generosity and sacrifice.)*

Remember that Jesus was a poor man himself. He grew up in a poor home (in which His mother was a poor widow, apparently) and lived with "no place to lay his head" (Matthew 8:20).

Taking the Next Step

Responding to Stories, 10-15 minutes

Distribute photocopies of Resource Sheet 7B, "The Reluctant Heart versus The Generous Heart." Read the first section and ask, "In what situations are we most likely to say, 'But it would cost me too much to do this . . .'? Let's think of some examples. Here are a few to get you going:"

    a. When you're going through financial difficulties, giving anything can be hard.

    b. Sometimes you get a large check from a project or from income tax; you plan to give a big chunk of it away. But as time passes, you think of other things that could be done with the money until that chunk shrinks to almost nothing.

    c. When it seems like you're on every mailing list, it's easy to feel put upon.

    Ask, "When, however, have you sacrificed with great joy?" Encourage sharing.

    Read the second section and ask, "In what situations are we most likely to say, 'But my gift is so small it wouldn't matter . . .'? Let's think of some examples."

    a. When you hear about a huge need—children starving or thousands dying.

    b. When you see others being generous—"A lot of people are giving to help that young girl go on a mission trip, so I don't need to."

    Ask, "When, however, have you seen God multiply a gift, or use a small gift to encourage someone in an incredible way?"

    The second story on the resource sheet points out how western money is automatically multiplied the minute it's sent to a Third World country. You may also wish to refer to the introductory story to Lesson 6.

    Read the third section and ask, "In what situations are we most likely to say, 'But it seems like a silly gift . . .'? Let's think of some examples."

    a. Gifts of great sentimentality can seem that way (see the last story on the sheet), but they are often valued more than other gifts.

    b. When someone asks you for a specific gift, you might be tempted to judge it as a foolish thing to give, but perhaps it is meaningful to the recipient.

    Ask, "When have you valued the thought behind a gift much more than the actual gift itself?" These are often gifts from children, grandchildren or students.

OPTION **Key Words, 5-7 minutes**

    Distribute photocopies of Resource Sheet 7B, "The Reluctant Heart versus The Generous Heart." Say to class members, "As this is read aloud, be open to what you need to hear regarding a generous heart. When a word or phrase touches you, underline it." Ask three volunteers to read one section each.

    Then ask, "What words or phrases did you underline? Why?" Allow people to share. When it's appropriate, ask, "What is needed to have a generous heart?"

Plan Two **Groups**

Building Community

    Tell about someone you know who has a generous heart. What differences can exist between a giver of gifts and someone with a generous heart? When has your own generous heart surprised you?

Considering Scripture

Read Luke 21:1-4.

    Who was Jesus with as He made this comment? (See Luke 20:45; 21:1, 3.)

    Jesus was making use of a teachable moment. Can you think of other times He did this? *(When they passed the fig tree that wasn't bearing fruit and He spoke of the uselessness of it and cursed it, Mark 11:12-14, 20; when they walked by the temple and He spoke of it—really his body—being torn down and rebuilt in three days, John 2:19.)*

Reproducible sheets:
Resource Sheet 7B

What doubts might this widow have had about putting all of her money in the temple offering?

Jesus had a habit of taking obvious truth and reversing it. In what way did He do this as He spoke to the disciples? *(It was obvious that the rich people gave more than the widow, but Jesus reversed it.)*

Why do you think Jesus would say that a person who gave less than a penny's worth (Mark 12:42) "put in more than all the others"?

What words in this passage let us know that this woman had no other money to live on?

In what other way had Jesus just defended poor widows? *(See the final verses of Luke 20.)*

OPTION

With what other poor widow was Jesus very familiar, perhaps giving Him a key to this woman's heart? *(His mother, Mary.)*

Taking the Next Step

1. The King James Version refers to the widow's money as the "widow's mite." It's been said this story isn't so much about the "widow's mite" as the "widow's might." In what way is this true?
2. What sort of character or knowledge or assurance does a person need to have in order to have a generous heart? *(An assurance of God's care and a joyful participation in the generous personality of God.)*

OPTION

Distribute photocopies of Resource Sheet 7B, "The Reluctant Heart versus The Generous Heart" and ask a group member to read it.

3. Look at the sentences that appear three times after the words, "The Reluctant Heart." Which of these problems of the reluctant heart is most familiar to you?
4. Pick one of these reluctant heart attitudes and read what comes after the corresponding "The Generous Heart." Ask, "What other truths answer this sort of reluctance?"

OPTION **Accountability Partners**

Have accountability groups meet and talk about how they can be more generous from the heart. One thing that helps is to confess the ways they aren't generous from the heart and pray for each other. (Perhaps as you give this announcement, you'd like to read the second story on Transparency 7, "What Would You Say Next?" and ask how many identify.)

OPTION **Worship Ideas**

Read Psalm 36 together as an act of worship.
Song Suggestions:
"Make Me a Servant" by Kelly Willard
"Give of Your Best to the Master" by Howard B. Grose and Charlotte A. Barnard

OPTION **Memory Verse**

"All these people gave their gifts out of their wealth; but she out of her poverty put in all she had to live on" (Luke 21:4).

Fleeting Thoughts

[1]As he looked up, Jesus saw the rich putting their gifts into the temple treasury. [2]He also saw a poor widow put in two very small copper coins. [3]"I tell you the truth," he said, "this poor widow has put in more than all the others. [4]All these people gave their gifts out of their wealth; but she out of her poverty put in all she had to live on."   Luke 21:1-4

Look at the above story in detail. Perhaps the woman had second thoughts at different moments in the story; perhaps, not. If so, what do you think she might have thought

1   . . . when she was at home, counting her money and looking at her pantry? (Keep in mind Jesus' words in v. 4: "she put in all she had to live on.")

    a. What I could do instead of giving this money:

    b. Why I will give this money anyway:

2   . . . when she heard about the teachers of the law (strutting around in flowing robes, being greeted in the marketplace and given the best seats in the synagogue) who were "devour[ing] widows' houses"? (See Luke 20:47, the verse immediately before today's passage.)

    a. What I could do instead of giving this money:

    b. Why I will give this money anyway:

3   . . . when she arrived at the temple and saw the rich people throwing in their huge amounts and saw in her own palm "two very small copper coins, worth only a fraction of a penny" (Mark 12:42). (The money receptacles in the temple had large metal trumpet-shaped openings. When people threw their money into the bell of the trumpet, it rattled and jingled loudly.)

    a. What I could do instead of giving this money:

    b. Why I will give this money anyway:

The Reluctant Heart versus The Generous Heart

The Reluctant Heart: But it would cost me too much to do this . . .

The Generous Heart: Sacrifice makes the gift more special.

The Durer brothers, Albrecht and Albert, worked for their father who was a goldsmith. The father began to notice that they had great artistic talent and he wanted them to develop their skill and become artists. But the father could not afford to send them to school. The two brothers discussed what they might do. They finally decided that one of them would work in the mines to pay the way for the other to go to school and develop his artistic skill. Then that brother would return the favor. But which brother would go to school first? They flipped a coin. Albrecht won the coin toss. So Albrecht went off to school to study art, painting and sculpture.

After four years, Albrecht came home. As they sat together at dinner, Albrecht said to his brother Albert, "Now it's your turn. We can support you." But Albert looked up mournfully and held up his hands. Every one of his fingers had been broken at least once working in the mine. They were gnarled and could not do the fine work necessary for an artist. Albert said, "It's too late for me." But he told his brother, "You go, and you do it for both of us."

Albrecht appreciated Albert's sacrifice so much that he devised a tribute to his brother. You have probably all seen Albrecht Durer's sculpture called, "The Praying Hands." The hands in that sculpture are the gnarled hands of his brother, Albert—hands that sacrificed. That's what it takes—sacrificing what is precious to us. Maybe we would have never known the genius of Albrecht Durer if it hadn't been for the sacrifice of his brother, Albert.

The Reluctant Heart: But my gift is so small it wouldn't matter . . .

The Generous Heart: God magnifies even the smallest gift.

There once was a little girl who wanted to give something to missions. All she had was a penny so she mailed that penny to a missionary in what was then Burma (now Myanmar). The missionary in Burma thought it was kind of cute so he said, "I'll do something with it." He bought a tract with it and gave that tract to a chief of a tribe in Burma. The chief couldn't read, but was curious about what the tract said, so he walked over two hundred and fifty miles to find somebody who could translate it. He believed what was in the tract and brought back the ideas to his tribe. They later invited missionaries to come to that village—all because a little girl gave just a penny. It didn't seem like a big gift at the time, but God turned it into something huge.

The Reluctant Heart: But it seems like a silly gift . . .

The Generous Heart: God values the pure attitude of the heart behind the gift.

Stu Weber said that one of his sons felt that he was the low man on the totem pole in the family. Everyone else in the family had something about them that was significant, but this boy felt that he was insignificant. Because this son liked the outdoors, Stu Weber decided to give him a pocket knife. It was one of those knives that can do just about anything. All of a sudden this boy became quite a man of interest in the family. His self esteem was raised. On Stu Weber's birthday, he opened a present from this son and discovered that he had given back the very pocket knife that had brought him so much joy. Did Stu want to accept that gift? No, but he did, because he knew what it meant to his son to give back to his father what was most precious to him.

—excerpted from Mike Shannon, *Lighten Up!*

What Would You Say Next?

After the church service, a little boy told the pastor: "When I grow up, I'm going to give you some money."

"Well, thank you," the pastor replied, "but why?"

"Because my daddy says you're one of the poorest preachers we've ever had."

If you were the pastor, what could you possibly say next?

If you were the father standing nearby, what could you possibly say next?

A couple invited some people to dinner. At the table, the mother turned to their six-year-old daughter and said, "Would you like to say the blessing?"

"I wouldn't know what to say," she replied.

"Just say what you've heard Mommy say," the mother answered.

The daughter bowed her head and said, "Dear Lord, Why on earth did I invite all these people to dinner?"

If you were the guest, what could you possibly say next?

If you were the mother, what could you possibly say next?

Eight
Encourage Like Barnabas

BARNABAS WAS A MAN who was willing to vouch for someone else's character. It's risky business to be put on somebody's reference list. You do what you can do, but sometimes people let you down. It was no small thing for Barnabas to take Saul by the hand and lead him to meet the apostles. Seven years later, Barnabas brought Paul to Antioch and even put him on his staff as his associate minister. Barnabas was a man who was willing to mentor those who needed assistance.

When Barnabas first began to be an encourager, I'm sure he didn't know what would be the fruitful outcome of his work. I want to encourage you to be like Barnabas. Be a good person, filled with the Holy Spirit and with faith (Acts 11:24). We can all become sons and daughters of encouragement.

—Mike Shannon, *Lighten Up!*

Central Theme: Shining like Jesus involves being an encourager in extremely practical ways: giving, mentoring, and coming alongside those who have failed, those who have been excluded, even those who once declared themselves to be our enemies.

Lesson Aim: Group members will examine the concrete ways in which Barnabas encouraged people and discuss what such behavior would look like in their everyday lives.

Bible Background: Acts 4:32-37; 9:26-28; 11:22-26; 15:37

For Further Study: Read Chapter 8 of *Lighten Up!*

Plan One **Classes**

Building Community

Materials you'll need for this session:
Resource Sheets 8A-8B, Transparency 8, pens or pencils, chalk and chalkboard.

Sentence Completion, 5-10 minutes

Display Transparency 8, "A Day in the Life of Barney," and say, "Let's look at a typical day in the life of Barney. He has several decisions to make. Let's give him a few more options than are listed on the sheet." Read the first situation and encourage class members to come up with several more options. At some point ask, "What would Barney do if he chose to be an encouraging person?" Do the same with the other situations.

OPTION Encourager of the Year Award, 5-10 minutes

Introduction: "Let's consider for a moment the people in our church. Who would you say deserves the award for 'Encourager of the Year'? Keep in mind that encouragement goes beyond superficial statements and gestures to include substantial service." To avoid competition of any kind, you may want to focus on people outside the class. If competition does develop, concede that your church is one of those that has many deserving recipients. Shift the focus from competition to character by asking,

"Why did you pick that person?" This will foster the telling of positive stories about each other.

Considering Scripture

Theme Search, 10-15 minutes

Distribute photocopies of Resource Sheet 8A, "Search for Encouragement" and say to class members, "As I read each passage aloud, underline any words that show Barnabas's pro-active ways of encouraging people. At the end of each passage, I'll give you a moment to write a few words to describe Barnabas's specific method or methods of encouragement."

Do the first one together. Read passage 1 and say something like, "Perhaps you underlined the last line, 'sold a field he owned and brought the money and put it at the apostles' feet.' The specific method of encouragement was Barnabas' willingness to give up land and money. He gave gifts to God that were useful to others."
Other possible answers include:
2. Underlined words: "Barnabas took [Saul] and brought him to the apostles." Method: Barnabas came alongside a "supposed" enemy, Saul who had killed Christians before his conversion.
3. Underlined words: "Barnabas went to Tarsus to look for Saul, and when he found him, he brought him to Antioch. So for a whole year Barnabas and Saul met with the church and taught great numbers of people." Method: Barnabas encouraged someone who had been excluded.
4. Underlined words: "Barnabas took Mark and sailed for Cyprus." Method: Barnabas gave second chances to those who failed.
In 2-4, some might add that Barnabas mentored both Saul (Paul) and then John Mark.

OPTION Matching, 10-15 minutes

Distribute photocopies of Resource Sheet 8A, "Search for Encouragement" and Resource Sheet 8B, "Barnabas, the Encourager." Read each passage of Scripture on Resource Sheet 8A aloud and then ask, Which of the four practical methods of encouragement listed in capital letters on Resource Sheet 8B do you find in this passage? As each heading on Resource Sheet 8B is suggested, ask someone to read the paragraph under it. Possible answers are found in the previous activity.

OPTION Subtitles, 10-12 minutes

Write on the chalkboard: "Barnabas . . ." Explain, "Our Scripture today is in four short sections. After we read each section, help me come up with a three-to five-word subtitle for the passage. To make it even easier, the first word in each subtitle is already supplied for you: Barnabas."

After you read each passage (Acts 4:32-37; 9:26-28; 11:22-26; 15:37), stop and ask class members to help you come up with the subtitle. Possibilities include: Barnabas gave land to help; Barnabas brought Saul to apostles; Barnabas teamed with Paul; Barnabas mentored Mark.

Ask, "In what specific ways was Barnabas an encourager?"

Taking the Next Step

Self Evaluation, 5-8 minutes

Ask four volunteers to read the different sections of Resource Sheet 8B, "Barnabas, the Encourager." Then ask, "Which story or comment speaks to you? Which of these methods of encouragement have you overlooked? Circle that one. Which one have you tried to do consistently and you need to keep doing it? Put a star by it."

OPTION **Sharing Questions, 10-15 minutes**

Distribute photocopies of Resource Sheet 8B, "Barnabas, the Encourager" and ask a volunteer to read the first paragraph aloud. Then ask, "When have you seen this done? When have you seen someone give an extraordinary gift that encouraged others deeply?"

Second paragraph: "When have you seen someone befriend and help another person who has treated him or her badly?"

Third paragraph: "When have you seen someone take someone under her wing who has been excluded, put down or minimized?"

Fourth paragraph: "When have you seen someone give a second chance to another person who failed?"

OPTION **Creative Expression, 10-15 minutes**

Distribute photocopies of Resource Sheet 8B, "Barnabas, the Encourager" and ask a volunteer to read it aloud. Then say, "Let's explore these specific ways of encouragement with creative expression. Pick one of the two following suggestions and feel free to work alone or with a partner."

Song Writing: Use the paragraph subtitles and ideas and put these words to the music of a song you know, perhaps a country-western song.

Pantomime: Figure out how you and someone else can pantomime one of the ideas on the resource sheet.

Allow time for the groups to work. If someone seems to particularly dislike these two suggestions, encourage them to come up with a creative expression of their own. In this case, it isn't necessary for groups to share what they've done.

Plan Two **Groups**

Building Community

Reproducible sheets:
Resource Sheet 8B
(optional)

"Think about the last time you were encouraged. How did that happen?" As group members give answers, write them on the board or chart. Then ask, "In which of these ways are you most likely to encourage someone?"

- Send a note
- Make a call
- Do a favor
- Send an anonymous gift
- (Others)

OPTIONAL QUESTION

Why do all sorts of people (even those who seem most confident) need encouragement?

Considering Scripture

Read Acts 4:32-37.

"In what way did Barnabas offer encouragement in this passage?

Whom exactly did he encourage?" *(Not only the needy, but others were probably encouraged to give by his gift.)*

Read Acts 9:26-28.

"How do you explain the fear of the disciples?" *(Saul had been the ruthless killer of Christians.)*

"How exactly did Barnabas encourage Saul?"

"Why was Barnabas' testimony about Saul so important to the apostles?" *(Barnabas was validating Saul's character and showing that what Saul said was true. They believed Barnabas because he had already proven his integrity and love.)*

Read Acts 11:22-26.

"What character qualities of Barnabas are mentioned here?"

"In what ways was Barnabas pro-active in his encouragement of Saul?"

Read Acts 15:37.

"Who was Barnabas encouraging in this chapter? How?"

"Why is it ironic that Paul did not give Mark a second chance?" *(Barnabas showed grace to Paul when others hadn't. Mention that Paul eventually did. See 2 Timothy 4:11.)*

OPTION

What odd thing happened in the relationship between Barnabas and Paul and how did Barnabas respond to it? Compare the wording of Acts 11:26, 30; 12:25; 13:2, 7 with Acts 13:42, 43, 46, 50; 14:1, 2, 23; 15:2, 22, 35. *(In all these passages, Barnabas and Paul's names are mentioned. In the earlier verses, Barnabas is mentioned first, indicating he was recognized to have greater importance. In the second group of passages, Paul's name comes first, indicating that things had changed and Paul had become more prominent. Yet Barnabas continued to be Paul's partner.)*

Taking the Next Step

1. In what specific ways did Barnabas encourage people? (See Resource Sheet 8B, "Barnabas, the Encourager" for suggested answers. Distribute photocopies of it, if you like.)
2. These methods show that encouragement is more than just talk. It involves going out of our way to do things for people. What are some examples of encouragement you've seen that are more than talk?
3. Who do you know who needs encouragement?

OPTION

4. Ask group members to shut their eyes for a moment and ponder the person's name that came to them in question 3. Urge them to ask God, "In what substantive ways could I encourage that person?"

OPTION **Accountability Partners**

Have partners meet and look at the ways God is already calling them to serve and ask themselves, "In these capacities, who am I being challenged to encourage?"

OPTION **Worship Ideas**

Read Psalm 41 together as an act of worship.

Song Suggestions:

"As We Gather" by Tommy Coombs

"God With Us" by Graham Kendrick

OPTION **Memory Verse**

Then Barnabas went to Tarsus to look for Saul, and when he found him, he brought him to Antioch. So for a whole year Barnabas and Saul met with the church and taught great numbers of people. The disciples were called Christians first at Antioch (Acts 11:25, 26).

Search for Encouragement

1. All the believers were one in heart and mind. No one claimed that any of his possessions was his own, but they shared everything they had. With great power the apostles continued to testify to the resurrection of the Lord Jesus, and much grace was upon them all. There were no needy persons among them. For from time to time those who owned lands or houses sold them, brought the money from the sales and put it at the apostles' feet, and it was distributed to anyone as he had need. Joseph, a Levite from Cyprus, whom the apostles called Barnabas (which means Son of Encouragement), sold a field he owned and brought the money and put it at the apostles' feet (Acts 4:32-37).

Specific Method(s) of Encouragement:

2. When [Saul] came to Jerusalem, he tried to join the disciples, but they were all afraid of him, not believing that he really was a disciple. But Barnabas took him and brought him to the apostles. He told them how Saul on his journey had seen the Lord and that the Lord had spoken to him, and how in Damascus he had preached fearlessly in the name of Jesus. So Saul stayed with them and moved about freely in Jerusalem, speaking boldly in the name of the Lord (Acts 9:26-28).

Specific Method(s) of Encouragement:

3. When he arrived and saw the evidence of the grace of God, he was glad and encouraged them all to remain true to the Lord with all their hearts. He was a good man, full of the Holy Spirit and faith, and a great number of people were brought to the Lord. Then Barnabas went to Tarsus to look for Saul, and when he found him, he brought him to Antioch. So for a whole year Barnabas and Saul met with the church and taught great numbers of people. The disciples were called Christians first at Antioch (Acts 11:22-26).

Specific Method(s) of Encouragement:

4. Barnabas wanted to take John, also called Mark with them, but Paul did not think it wise to take him, because he had deserted them in Pamphylia and had not continued with them in the work. They had such a sharp disagreement that they parted company. Barnabas took Mark and sailed for Cyprus, but Paul chose Silas and left, commended by the brothers to the grace of the Lord (Acts 15: 37).

Specific Method(s) of Encouragement:

Barnabas, the Encourager

GIVER OF GIFTS

Jesus, who told us to go into the world and preach the gospel, also told us to give a cup of cold water, to clothe those who are naked, and to visit those who are in prison (Matthew 10:42; 25:31-46). Anyone who takes the Bible seriously should also take these commandments as seriously as Barnabas did.

COMING ALONGSIDE A "SUPPOSED" ENEMY

In the book, *The Other Twelve,* Leslie Flynn compares Saul to Charles Colson. When Colson first became a Christian, people didn't know whether to accept him or not. When he been known as Nixon's hatchet man, he was a tough man, often involved in dirty tricks. Then Harold Hughes invited Charles Colson to his Bible study and prayer group. While there, Colson saw a man he had once played a dirty trick on. Harold Hughes gave a testimony about giving up hatred. He said, "One man I used to hate was Charles Colson, but I have brought him to you today as a Christian brother and I want you to welcome him." At the end of the Bible study, the man Colson had played the dirty trick on was asked to pray. He came over and grasped Colson's hand as they formed a prayer circle. Colson recalls what an extraordinary experience it was to be accepted into that circle. But it never would have happened if Harold Hughes had not had the courage to be a Barnabas and bring him in.

ENCOURAGING THOSE WHO HAVE BEEN EXCLUDED

Perhaps you've heard this story about the early days of the Billy Graham crusades. Sometimes the crusade would go into a city where segregation was the law. Blacks and whites could not sit together. Rather than challenge segregation or not go at all, Billy Graham would schedule the crusade but right before the meeting he would personally walk through the crowd and remove the barriers. Who was going to tell him he couldn't? In that way, he was telling people who had been shut out and treated as outcasts that they were accepted by God.

GIVING SECOND CHANCES TO THOSE WHO FAIL

I had a tough time in one of my early ministries. I felt people weren't responding well and I got a lot of criticism. I decided to leave the ministry. I wrote my resignation letter and brought it to the chairman of the elders. He very quietly read my letter and then, without saying a word, he folded it, tore it up and threw it in the trash can. He said, "I refuse to accept this letter. If we're not responding to the preaching of the Word, it's our fault, not yours. If you want to find another church, find another church. If you want to stay with us, stay with us. But don't leave the ministry." The elder continued, "Don't leave a mark like that on the record of this church. We don't want to drive a good man out of the ministry." People like him were in my life whenever I needed that kind of encouragement—the kind that Barnabas offered.

All of us need someone like Barnabas—need someone who is willing to believe in us. I experienced that in high school when I was very insecure. I tried sports. I wasn't good at sports. I tried to get elected to office. I lost the election. I was really floundering. What was I going to do? Then a drama teacher saw potential in me and cast me for a major role in the first play I ever auditioned for. That flabbergasted me, but I gave it my best. I ended up being in drama for the rest of my high school and college career. This drama teacher helped me acquire the confidence that otherwise I would not have had.

—excerpted from Mike Shannon, *Lighten Up!*

A Day in the Life of Barney

7:31 AM

Barney got up, shaved, and got dressed. As he started out to the car, he saw his neighbor outside and remembered the neighbor wanted to borrow a tool. So Barney . . .
- went out and greeted him.
- hid in his house until the neighbor went indoors and then hurried out to his car.
- other: (Have some fun with this.)

8:05 AM

Barney went to his office, but noticed that nasty Gertrude was by the water cooler. She had reported him for an infraction (which everyone deemed as an unfair one), and he couldn't stand her. Just yesterday, she was reported for that same infraction and it looked like she could use some sympathy. So Barney . . .
- walked by quietly, but dreamed of yelling, NOW YOU KNOW HOW IT FEELS!
- waited for her to leave and then told the guy she'd been talking to how she'd turned him in.
- went to Gertrude and showed her just how wonderful he was by sympathetically listening to her story without bringing up what she had done to him.
- other: (Have more fun.)

11:53 AM

At lunch, Barney got ready to go out with the guys, but one of them invited a *woman* to come along. He wasn't keen on this because the guys enjoyed themselves so much. So Barney . . .
- didn't go to lunch with the guys.
- said it was fine for her to come, but hoped she would decide not to go.
- went to lunch, but didn't speak to her or look at her.
- went to lunch and asked her questions just to show what a special guy he is.
- other: (You know Barney by now—go for it.)

6:22 PM

Barney went home and found out his thirteen-year-old daughter had ditched school again. So Barney . . .
- grounded her for three and half years, then watched sports and tried not to think about how he felt like a failure as a parent.
- left it all to his wife.
- called his mother to hear about how wonderful he was when he was thirteen.
- other: (Be creative!)

Nine
Trust Like Rhoda

ALL WE KNOW of Rhoda is that she was a servant girl in the household of John Mark's family. Her life in that household must have been interesting, for we believe this was the house in which the disciples gathered for the upper room experience. It may also have been the house in which the Holy Spirit came upon the apostles. In Acts 12, we see that the church met together there to pray for Peter.

What a blow the imprisonment of Peter must have been after the church had just faced the severe loss of James, the apostle! To see Peter, another one of that inner circle of Jesus, the one who was "chairman of the executive committee" so to speak, in jail facing possible death must have been scary. Jesus was executed. James was executed. They had every reason to believe death would come to Peter too. And so they prayed.

—Mike Shannon, *Lighten Up!*

Central Theme: Being a disciple of Jesus means that we grow to trust God in the midst of difficult circumstances and accept His answers.

Lesson Aim: Group members will examine the simple trust of Rhoda and explore what it means to trust God to the point of acceptance.

Bible Background: Acts 12:1-25

For Further Study: Read Chapter 9 of *Lighten Up!*

Plan One **Classes**

Building Community

Mad-Lib, 5-8 minutes

Explain, "We're going to play mad-libs for a minute. I'll ask you to suggest words that fit certain parts of speech. I'll fill them in on the blank lines on the transparency and then I'll put it up for all of us to see."

Look for the blanks on Transparency 9, "Church Romance" and ask class members to suggest the words in parentheses below the blank lines. As they suggest them, write them in the blanks. Then display the transparency and read it for the class.

Close with this question: "Why is Margo having a hard time accepting this answer?"

OPTION Good News/Bad News Story, 5-8 minutes

Explain, "Let's try to come up with a good news/bad news story in which something looks good, but then it turns it bad. Then it looks bad, but it turns out good. Here is an example:

The bad news is: Craig's dream was to join an elite group in the military, but his asthma is so bad that he won't be accepted.

The good news is: He's just met a sweet girl whom he would never have wanted to have left behind. And—she works for the company he wants to work for!"

Materials you'll need for this session: Resource Sheets 9A, 9B, Transparency 9, pens or pencils, chalk and chalkboard.

Continue: The bad news is . . . the good news is . . .

If you wish, close with this question, "How can acceptance turn bad news into good news?"

Considering Scripture

Science "Experiment" Summary, 15-18 minutes

Distribute photocopies of Resource Sheet 9A, "Story Chemistry." Explain, "Today's passage has interesting 'chemistry' and we're going to see how the elements mix and what comes out of it. This handout will serve as the report on our experiment. I'll assign each of you (or pairs of you) certain portions of this report to fill out. Read the portion assigned to you and fill out your section of the report."

Assign each of the numbered questions to a group to answer. You may wish to assign questions five and six to the same group. Give class members a few minutes and ask them to report back. Here are some possible answers they might offer.

(1) Herod had just executed the apostle James. He had arrested Peter and planned to execute him. You may want to read the last paragraph of the introduction above.

(2) Peter was somehow relaxed enough to sleep bound in chains to two soldiers. He responded to the angel by thinking it was all a vision. "Odd" occurrences are numerous! A light shone in the cell, but this didn't wake Peter up so the angel struck him! The chains fell off Peter's wrists. The guards didn't stop Peter and the angel from leaving the city.

Peter finally concluded that he had been rescued (vs. 11).

(3) Rhoda believed the man at the door was Peter and faithfully announced him (although she forgot to invite him in, but left him standing at the door). Mention here the various things Rhoda may have experienced, as mentioned in the first paragraph of the introduction above. These experiences would imply that she also had met Jesus.

(4) The Christians not only didn't believe her, but they told her she was crazy. Then they came up with the idea that she had seen "Peter's angel," presumably Peter's guardian angel who somehow resembled him.

Read "The Outcome." and note how the Scripture provides a report of the outcome.

(5) The guards who had not noticed Peter and the angel walking by were executed (vs. 6, 10, 19).

(6) Herod left for Caesarea and then during a royal address, a crowd declared his voice was that of a god, which he didn't deny. God struck him down and he was eaten by worms.

OPTION Trust Thermometers, 12-15 minutes

On the chalkboard, write these words: Peter, Rhoda, the church. Under each one, draw a thermometer (two vertical lines with an almost enclosed circle at the bottom is good enough).

Before reading today's passage together aloud, say, "When we've finished reading the passage, we're going to chart the trust of each of these characters or sets of characters to see how 'warm' their trust in God was. How did each of them respond to God's miraculous release of Peter? So as we read, listen for cues about trust and lack of trust."

After the passage is read, stand near the "Peter" thermometer and ask class members, "How did Peter respond to his miraculous release?"

After that person has answered, give him a piece of chalk and ask them to make a mark on the thermometer. Then ask the same question again and after hearing an answer, ask if he would make his mark above or below the first one. Do the same with "Rhoda" and "the church," using information from the introduction if you like.

If time is short, cover only Acts 12:1-17.

OPTION Combination

After you go over the passage thoroughly with the Science "Experiment" Summary, use the trust thermometers to look at the trust of each character.

Key Word Search and Discussion, 10-15 minutes

Taking the Next Step

Distribute photocopies of Resource Sheet 9B, "Acceptance: The Key to Trusting God In Prayer." Explain, "The key to Rhoda's trust was that she—unlike Peter—didn't think she was having a vision! She didn't think the guy outside was Peter's angel. She knew she wasn't crazy either. She accepted exactly what she saw—Peter standing at the door with no chains.

Ask a volunteer or two to read the handout, but first say, "As we read this together, underline the words 'accept' and 'trust' whenever we come across them." (Afterward, note that they appear nine times.)

Ask these questions if you like:

"How are acceptance and trust related?" (*Acceptance makes it easier to trust.*)

"What happens within us when we don't accept the answers God gives?" (*We become bitter and disconnected to God.*)

Neighbor Nudge, 7-10 minutes

If you haven't already distributed photocopies of Resource Sheet 9B, "Acceptance: The Key to Trusting God In Prayer," do so now. Ask class members to choose a partner from whomever is seated around them. Then say to each class member, "You may have a prayer that seems unanswered to you or answered in a way that troubles you. Perhaps acceptance is the key. Try out this idea by thinking of such a situation and then telling your partner which of the points on the handout would help you accept the answer to prayer you have (or the seeming non-answer). Do not feel you have to say exactly what that prayer was. You may if you wish, but the important thing will be to verbalize to your partner how you could better accept and trust."

Allow a few minutes for partners to talk. Some may not feel comfortable sharing this information with their partners so don't allow them to feel pressured to state specifics.

Partnered Prayer, 3-5 minutes

Say to class members, "As partners, you've just honored each other with information about your relationship with God. Pray for each other now—aloud or silently—that acceptance and trust will grow."

Plan Two **Groups**

Building Community

Bring the Sunday newspaper comics with you and pass different pages around the group.

Ask, "What cartoon character or TV sitcom character finds it difficult to accept things—circumstances, people, self?"

"When is it difficult to accept success?" (*When it requires sacrifices, when you don't believe in yourself.*)

"What sorts of answers to prayer are difficult to accept?"

Materials needed:
Sunday newspaper comics

Considering Scripture

Read Acts 12:1-4, The Prologue

What three key names are mentioned in these verses?

How do you think the arrest of two out of three of the 'inner three' of Jesus' disciples affected the church?

Read Acts 12:5-17, The Drama

Why did the angel strike Peter? *(To wake him up. Note that the shining light hadn't been effective in waking Peter up.)*

How did the angel solve the problem of Peter being chained to two soldiers?

How did the angel solve the problem of the guards and the impassable city gate?

How did Peter respond to being let out of prison?

How did the church "thank" Rhoda for announcing Peter?

Who did they suggest might really be at the door in place of Peter?

What was Peter's response?

Read Acts 12:18-24, The Aftermath

What became of Herod?

Taking the Next Step

How do you account for the church having such a difficult time accepting Peter's release? *(They felt fear and intimidation from Herod.)*

How can we better imitate the simple acceptance of God's will that Rhoda modeled? *(She didn't make elaborate excuses for what might be happening. She first looked at the obvious answer and assumed God was in it.)*

How does simple acceptance of what God does—what we like and what we don't like—enhance our relationship with God? *(Non-acceptance often causes our relationship with God to break down in bitterness and despair. Acceptance builds trust. If you wish, distribute photocopies of Resource Sheet 9B, "Acceptance: The Key to Trusting God In Prayer."*

OPTION

In what area do you most need to trust God more by accepting what God is doing in that area?

OPTION **Accountability Partners**

Have accountability partners meet and further discuss question four in "Taking the Next Step." Ask them to pray for each other about this. If you wish, give them photocopies of Resource Sheet 9B, "Acceptance: The Key to Trusting God In Prayer" and urge them to use the subtitles to measure their level of acceptance.

OPTION **Worship Ideas**

Read Psalm 37 together as an act of worship.

Song Suggestions:

"Blessed Be the Lord God Almighty" by Bob Fitts

"Sure Foundation" by Don Harris

OPTION **Memory Verse**

"When she recognized Peter's voice, she was so overjoyed she ran back without opening it and exclaimed, 'Peter is at the door!'" (Acts 12:14)

Story Chemistry

Goal: To re-join two elements which were once joined: Peter and the church.

THE PRE-CONDITIONS (vs. 1-4)

    (1) What was the problem?
        What past events affected this one?

THE PRINCIPAL ELEMENTS: (vs. 5-15)

    (2) Peter:
        How did Peter respond to prison?

        How did Peter respond to the angel?

        What "odd" things happened (e.g. the gate opened by itself, vs. 10)?

        What did Peter finally conclude?

    (3) Rhoda:
        How did she respond to Peter's presence?

    (4) The Church:
        How did they respond to Rhoda?

THE OUTCOME: (vs. 16, 17)

But Peter kept on knocking, and when they opened the door and saw him, they were astonished. Peter motioned with his hand for them to be quiet and described how the Lord had brought him out of prison. "Tell James and the brothers about this," he said, and then he left for another place.

THE AFTERMATH: (vs. 18-25)

What happened concerning:

    (5) The guards:

    (6) Herod:

Acceptance: the Key to Trusting God in Prayer

ACCEPTANCE HELPS US . . .

SEE THE ANSWERS

In this instance, Rhoda was able to see an answer to the prayers of the church. She witnessed not just a church in community and in crisis, but also a church in prayer. She was no doubt praying herself and then she saw the church in triumph. This servant girl was willing to accept Peter's release more quickly than the leaders were. She received her answer with great joy.

STAY CONNECTED WITH GOD EVEN WHEN THE ANSWERS ARE DIFFICULT

Think of Jesus' prayer in Gethsemane: "My Father, if it is possible, may this cup be taken from me. Yet not as I will, but as you will" (Matthew 26:39). Jesus asked that He not have to endure the cross, but He did. Notice that Jesus phrased it this way, "if it is possible." We have to accept the fact that some things are not possible. I can accept that because I have a hard enough time running my own life without trying to run the universe.

In my own life, my wife and I have dealt with the pain of infertility. We prayed a lot to conceive children but it has never happened. On the other hand, a woman at a church where I served told me she was in great grief over her inability to conceive children and asked if I would give a special prayer for her. I did that and she has had three children since then. Sometimes I say, "Lord, I don't understand why you've granted my prayers for other people but you haven't granted them for me." I don't understand that. Now God has been kind to me in other ways. I don't understand that either. There are times when I need to sit back and say, "OK, God. I can't understand all these answers, but I know you love me."

RELY ON GOD TO COME THROUGH

A lot of us, I suppose, share the faith of a little child who was staying with her grandfather. He was happy to see her praying at night, kneeling by her bed. But the words coming out of her mouth were unusual. She was saying, A, B, C, D, E, F, G, H, I, J. When she finished praying, her grandfather said, "Honey I was glad to see you praying, but why were you reciting the alphabet?" She said, "I don't really know what to say, so I just say the letters and I let God put the words together." Sometimes that is exactly what we have to do. And we have to accept the fact that sometimes God says no.

RESPOND WITH JOY

I wish I had the trust Rhoda showed by the way she simply accepted God's answer with great joy. That's a childlike quality, isn't it? Jesus said that if we wanted to be great in the kingdom, we had to be like a little child (Matthew. 18:3, 4). So whether we learn trust from the chronological children among us or from the new believers, we need to develop the kind of trust that Rhoda had. This is the kind of trust that can handle any emergency and any outcome. This trust can bless Peter and bless James and believe that God used both events for His glory.

—excerpted from Mike Shannon, *Lighten Up!*

Church Romance

There once was a woman named Margo, who looked a lot like _____.

(female in room).

She was anxious to find a _____ boyfriend, but he didn't turn up.

(adjective)

When the church hired a new associate pastor, Margo joined the

_____. Margo and the new pastor, whose

(program at your church)

name was Harry, became friends, discussing _____

(adjective)

problems the group had, and trying to figure out ways to

_____ them. But the young fella, Harry,

(verb)

who looked a lot like _____ , was

(famous pre-1900 president)

shy and couldn't share his _____ feelings.

(adjective)

So Margo prayed every night and promised to trust God. Finally she confronted

Harry, saying, "_____ , how do you feel about me?" He gulped

(term of endearment)

and said he had to practice his _____. She cried for _____

(musical instrument)   *(number)*

hours in the church bathroom. Finally, when she came out, Harry was playing the

song, _____. Harry adjusted his glasses

(popular love song)

glasses and his eyes said, "That song is for you." That was what she wanted to hear.

Should she trust the answer?

Ten
Take a Stand Like Paul

PAUL'S CONVERSION CAUSED HIM to take a stand for Christ—opposite to his previous one. The enemy and chief persecutor of the church became its chief missionary. He began to see himself as a minister of Christ instead of as an opponent of Christ. He saw himself as a minister to people he had formerly despised. This man who considered himself the pinnacle of Judaism and a Pharisee of the Pharisees started preaching to Gentiles and telling them they could become Christians directly without becoming Jews first. Paul received a lot of opposition and mistreatment for that position, but he stood up for it. Formerly, he would have despised and kept himself from Gentiles, but when he became a Christian, they became his mission.

—adapted from Mike Shannon, *Lighten Up!*

Central Theme: Standing up for Christ often involves moving in the opposite direction you've been going. It requires that you be open to the nudges and realizations God sends your way.
Lesson Aim: Group members will examine how God prompted Paul to change his life and follow God's purposes, and we can respond to God's radical nudges in a similar way.
Bible Background: Acts 9:1-22; 26:13-18
For Further Study: Read Chapter 10 of *Lighten Up!*

Plan One **Classes**

Building Community

Materials you'll need for this session:
Resource Sheets 10A, 10B, Transparency 10, pens or pencils, chalk and chalkboard.

Respond to an Anecdote

Read the following anecdote:

"You may remember that the late George Wallace, the former governor of Alabama was known in his earlier days as a proponent of segregation as well as racism. After he was shot and paralyzed and faced his own struggles, he began to realize what suffering was like. One day George Wallace wheeled his wheelchair into a Montgomery, Alabama church that was predominantly African-American and asked for the forgiveness of those people. He asked them to forgive the pain he had caused them and they forgave him. He dedicated the latter part of his life to reconciliation."

Ask this question, "We know what happened to this man's body—it was paralyzed, but what happens in the heart of a person to cause such a dramatic change?" You may want to point out that not everyone who becomes disabled makes such a change. The key is the change of heart, not the tragedy. (There was a repentance and a coming to one's self.)

OPTION **Sharing Contest, 5-8 minutes**

Before class, choose three people to be judges. Choose three who are as different as possible from each other—gender, type of work, type of personality. Bring paper and pencil for them.

In class, say to your adults, "Think for a moment about a dramatic change you've made recently. It doesn't have to be seriously dramatic. It could be, for instance, that you starting eating avocados at the age of fifty or that you began saying, 'I love you,' to your aging mother. After you've thought of changes you've made, we want to hear them."

After giving them a moment to think, ask them for their answers. Explain that the judges will give each answer a number from 1-10, based on the degree of change required, or drama involved. After everyone has shared their ideas, see which class member(s) wins with the highest score.

Before & After Chart, 10-15 minutes

Ask class members to form small groups of four or five and distribute photocopies of Resource Sheet 10A, "Before and After Paul's Conversion" to each class member. Say to class members, "When the apostle Paul was converted, he made an opposite turn in his life from the way he was heading. Not only did he change his course, but he followed his new course with the same energy he followed the old. Let's look at that change of course. As a group, fill out each section of this chart, noting the differences in his life in each area."

To help with clarity in this long passage of Scripture, you may want to read aloud Acts 8:1-4; 9:1-2 as a large group, identifying it clearly as the "BEFORE" Scripture, and then say, "This is what Saul was like before his conversion. In your groups, read Acts 9:3-22 and Acts 26:12-18." (This second passage in chapter 26 is a similar account in which Paul retold his experience to a different audience, but he included a few more details about God's message to him.) Then fill out each section of the chart.

Circulate among the groups making sure they're picking up the major points. If possible, call them together after a few minutes and summarize this way:

Ethnic attitudes *before:* Saul was a zealous Jew, a killer of Christians. He was also a Pharisee, which meant he despised Gentiles even more than other Jews. *After* his conversion, Paul became an apostle specifically to the Gentiles.

Thoughts about Jesus Christ *before:* Saul viewed Him as a false messiah whose followers must be executed. *After:* Paul spoke with Jesus and recognized Him as Lord and Messiah.

Views on the church *before:* He believed it to be a heretical sect that must be demolished. *After:* He saw them as the people of God who must be nurtured.

Views about himself *before:* He thought he was right to kill people defiling God's cause. *After:* He saw that he had sinned against God by persecuting Christians.

Thoughts about his mission in life *before:* to carry out the letter of the law according to Judaism. *After:* to help Gentiles find Christ and establish churches to nurture them.

OPTION Dramatic Monologues, 5-8 minutes

Distribute photocopies of Resource Sheet 10A, "Before and After Paul's Conversion" to each class member and work through it together as a large group, reading the passages and asking class members for input. Early in the discussion, say, "As we do this, consider wrapping all this up by giving us an impromptu monologue as Paul, either before his conversion or after. In that monologue, you'll need to cover the basic points in the left column. Your first sentence will be: I am Paul, before my conversion. This is how I felt about . . ."

After you've worked through the chart, ask for volunteers by saying, "Who would like to give a monologue as Paul?" Repeat the first sentence from above. Give them a few minutes to respond.

Considering Scripture

OPTION 5-8 minutes

Distribute photocopies of Resource Sheet 10B, "Being Open to Realizations from God." Ask a volunteer to read the first section and then ask these questions:

"What were some of the things God may have used as nudges (or goads) to help Saul come to his sudden realization of Christ?" *(The vision, Stephen's response when stoned; Gamaliel's hands-off, "God will lead" approach toward curbing Christianity; the behavior of the persecuted Christians.)*

"What usually causes people to come to themselves?"

Taking the Next Step

Fill in the Details of the Story, 10-15 minutes

Display Transparency 10, "How Chuck Gets a Heart for God" and read the opening paragraph. Then ask the first question: "What 180 degree turn would God love to see in this man?" *(Understanding the chief task of the church: to love as Christ did, to make disciples, to witness to the community.)*

Ask class members to move into small groups of five and give them paper and pencils. Say, "Now that we've established the setting and the problem of the story, finish it, using the other two questions to help you do that. If you get stuck with the story line, refer back to these. Along the way, feel free to add character, traumatic events, conversations to the story. Try to complete this in ten minutes."

If time permits, ask groups to share their stories.

OPTION Letters from Screwtape, 5-8 minutes

Say to class members, "In C.S. Lewis' classic novel, *The Screwtape Letters*, a senior devil makes suggestions to a junior devil about how to capture a certain person for the evil side, using subtle methods. Let's try to imagine how such a letter would be written about you in this light."

"What radical changes would your not-so-guardian devil NOT want you to make?"

"What nudges from God would your not-so-guardian devil want you to ignore?"

"In what ways would your not-so-guardian devil NOT want you to see yourself?"

Letters to God 5-8 minutes

If you haven't already distributed Resource Sheet 10B, "Being Open to Realizations from God," do so now. Have someone read it aloud and say, "Turn this sheet over and write your own letter to God. Be sure to mention these two things: the nudges God may have been giving you and the way God is helping you see your true self."

Plan Two **Groups**

Building Community

What is the biggest change you've made recently? (This doesn't have to be serious. Simple changes can be a big deal to the participant.)

How do you rate yourself regarding change?
- I love change.
- I like change occasionally.
- I endure change.
- I detest change.

"Who do you know who needs to make a 180 degree turn in her life in some way—only she think she's doing the right thing?" (Point out later this was Paul's predicament.)

Read Acts 9:1-9.

What were the drives and motives of Paul (Saul) at the beginning of this passage? (Refer also to Acts 8:1-4 for more details.)

What physical changes and movement happened to Saul and to the men he was with? (*Saul fell down and was struck blind. The men with him were speechless. Saul did not eat or drink for three days.*)

By what title did Saul address the voice of Jesus, whom he seemed to recognize? (*He called Jesus "Lord," even though he had previously persecuted people who had stated that truth.*)

Read Acts 9:10-22.

Why would Ananias have had great reasons not to help Saul?

What purpose had God already carved out for Saul, who would be Paul? (*See v. 15.*)

God could have given Saul his sight back at any time. Why was it so important to involve Ananias in the healing process?

How did Saul baffle his old friends, the Jews?

Read Acts 26:13-18

In verse 14, the voice of Jesus said that it was difficult for Saul to keep resisting divine nudges and promptings to change ("It is hard for you to kick against the goads.") From what you know of Saul's history, what might some of them have been? (You may wish to prompt group members with information and references from Resource Sheet 10B, "Being Open to Realizations from God.")

Considering Scripture

Saul, like the prodigal son, "came to himself" (Luke 15:17, KJV). What usually causes people to come to themselves (since it's usually not a vision from Heaven!)? (*Crises, failure, burnout; insightful words of a friend, relative or even a child.*)

Many of Saul's nudges from God seem to come from people—those he persecuted, in fact. Who is God most likely to use to nudge you into seeing how your life needs to change?

In what areas of your life does a 180 degree turn need to be made?

Taking the Next Step

OPTION **Accountability Partners**

Have accountability groups meet and ask them to discuss question three in "Taking the Next Step." If they wish to be more specific about what the turn is, urge them to do so. If all they're willing to discuss is the area that needs change, that's fine.

OPTION **Worship Ideas**

Read 2 Timothy 4:1-2 as closing act of worship.
Song Suggestions:
"Mourning Into Dancing" by Tommy Walker
"Change My Heart, O God" by Eddie Espinosa

OPTION **Memory Verse**

"We all fell to the ground, and I heard a voice saying to me in Aramaic, 'Saul, Saul, why do you persecute me? It is hard for you to kick against the goads'" (Acts 26:14).

Before and After Paul's Conversion

	BEFORE Acts 8:1-4; 9:1, 2	AFTER Acts 9:3-22; 26:12-18
ethnic attitudes		
thoughts about Jesus Christ		
views on the church		
views on himself		
thoughts about his mission in life		

Being Open to Realizations From God

GOD'S PART—SENDING THE NUDGES

Saul's conversion may seem like a sudden one, but when Paul told the story later, he recounted that one of the things Jesus said to him was, "It is hard for you to kick against the goads" (Acts 26:14). In other words, "I've been trying to prod you, or to use a goad to move you in the right direction, but you've been resisting." Later, Paul said that this event was not so much for his conversion as for his commission. (Acts 26:16). That great light on the road to Damascus may have blinded Paul, but it helped him to see things he had never seen before.

Besides the vision, which was of course a significant nudge, I wonder if the death of Stephen might have been a goad as well. Saul held the coats of the men who stoned Stephen to death (Acts 7:54–8:1). Perhaps the attitude of Stephen—the brightness of his countenance, his courage, his peace—began to affect him.

There was also the influence of his mentor, Gamaliel. Saul had studied to be a rabbi under Gamaliel, the most famous teacher of his day. When Peter and the other apostles were on trial for preaching in the temple courts, Gamaliel warned the Sanhedrin to leave them alone. He said, ". . . If their purpose or activity is of human origin, it will fail. But if it is from God, you will not be able to stop these men" (Acts 5:34-39). Don't you imagine that Gamaliel's warning shook the foundations of Saul's position against the church?

What about the example of all the people Saul had persecuted? Paul later affirmed that he had been responsible for the deaths of some Christians (Acts 26:9-11; 1 Timothy 1:13, 15, 16). Don't you imagine the commitment and courage of those he persecuted affected him? Maybe he began to think he wasn't their superior after all, but that they were his superiors. He saw that he was not the man he wanted to be and that was a painful truth to discover.

OUR PART—SEEING OUR TRUE SELVES

The prodigal son had a sudden realization too. He spent all of his money on riotous living and then found he no friends left either. The only job he could find was feeding the pigs. He got so hungry he began to envy the pigs and wished he could eat what they ate. The Bible says, "He came to himself" (Luke 15:17, KJV). When he came to himself, he decided to go home. He decided it was better to be a servant in his father's house than to be free in the place he was.

Saul came to himself and could see himself better. He sensed, "I'm on the wrong side. I'm on the wrong road. I'm playing for the wrong team." Saul was always zealous for God. He was never a selfish or lazy person. He had been serving God to the best of his knowledge prior to this, but he had gotten it wrong about Jesus. That's a tough thing to recognize. It's always tough to recognize that even though we've been serving the Lord, we've been doing it the wrong way.

Have you ever at some time in your life felt you were not the person you wanted to be—that you hadn't done what you had intended to do? To be disappointed with aspects of your life is a painful thing. We can't go back and change the things that we have done or not done. But, like Paul, we can also become the subject of forgiveness. For along with the pain and the knowledge of what Paul had done came the beautiful message of grace. Paul learned this message well enough that he was able to articulate effectively for the rest of his life. We can also take hold of this grace

—adapted from Mike Shannon, *Lighten Up!*

How Chuck Gets a Heart for God

Chuck's goal is to make sure this church is run right! He wants everything done "the correct way" and when it's not, he can very unpleasant and conniving. Still, he loves God so he does pray for all these people who don't understand how a church ought to operate.

What 180 degree turn would God love to see in this man?

What nudges might God give this man?

How does this man need to see himself?